Electronic Corpse

Poems from a Digital Salon

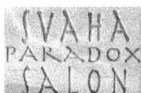

Electronic Corpse

Poems from a Digital Salon

◊◊◊

M. Ayodele Heath, Editor

SVAHA PARADOX SALON

Copyright ©2014 by M. Ayodele Heath

All rights reserved. No part of this book may be reproduced or republished without written consent from the publisher, except by reviewers who may quote brief excerpts in connection with a review in a newspaper, magazine, or electronic publication; nor may any part of this book be reproduced, stored in a retrieval system, or transmitted in any form, or by any means recorded without written consent of the publisher.

Svaha Paradox Salon
Pittsburgh, PA
thesvahaparadox@gmail.com
http://www.christinaspringer.com

Electronic Corpse: Poems from a Digital Salon

ISBN-10:   0-615-95420-0
ISBN-13:   978-0-615-95420-2

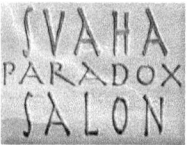

Cover Design:	Krista Franklin (http://www.kristafranklin.com/)
Cover Layout:	Stephen H. Segal (http://stephenhsegal.com) Christina Springer
Internal Art Design:	Christina Springer
Copy Editing:	Jaime McClung Christina Springer
Layout:	Norman Nunley, Jr.

TABLE OF CONTENTS

INTRODUCTION BY YONA HARVEY .... *I*
FOREWORD BY CHRISTINA SPRINGER .... *III*
A LETTER FROM THE EDITOR BY M. AYODELE HEATH .... *V*

I. THE CONSCIOUSNESSES

#67: We keep coming to this part 3
#115: Japanese scientists unveiled a robot that plays the violin 4
#19: This dream of water—what does it harbor 5
#87: The five cool stars above this town 6
#80: The winter her body no longer fit 7
#55: They named me something French 8
#10: Once I pried open my doll's head 9
#105: If Kali were a car, what kind of car would she be 10
#143: When I heard the bombing 11
#23: Luxury, then, is a way of 12

II. VOICE LESSONS

#57: The hardest part about 15
#33: I've included this letter in the group 16
#44: God of breathing 17
#1: The small dog barking at the darkness has something to say 18
#135: In this country you may not 19
#53: One voice can change a room 20
#69: Yesterday a man was sucked out of an airplane over the blue-tipped mountains .. 21
#75: A child said, what is the grass? 22
#63: "Man invented language to satisfy his deep need to complain." 23
#61: Because I am a girl, no one knows my birthday 24

III. LOVE, COBOL, & OTHER FORGOTTEN LANGUAGES

#62: First, are you our sort of a person? 26
#28: Everything measured. A man twists 27
#43: Both of them were history, even before one 28
#138: We married for acceptance: to stall the nagging 29
#36: In an effort to get people to look into each other's eyes more 30
#131: Above us, stars. Beneath us, constellations. 31
#12: The night is fractured and they shiver, blue, those stars, in the distance .. 32
#125: Here am I floating 33

    #133: Difficulties break some men but make others … 34
    #3: The day came fat with an apple in its mouth … 35
    #17: I got news yesterday … 36
    #94: Like streetlights … 37
    #139: If this life is all we have … 38

IV. ANIMATION

    #60: We write to taste life twice – in the moment and in retrospect … 41
    #24: The trouble is, you can never take … 42
    #72: Ladies and gentlemen, ghosts and children of the state … 43
    #93: These hands will never forget the prickling touch … 44
    #32: Turns out the radiologist didn't know thing one about radios … 45
    #64: What if you knew you'd be the last … 46
    #130: When we grew up and went to school … 47
    #41: I think it is interesting, though not exactly amusing … 48
    #66: A friend asks, "What was at stake for you in the Eighties?" … 49
    #126: Most animals can't … 50

V. I-MAKING & MINE-MAKING: A PARADOX

    #141: A man is walking toward me … 53
    #144: Just as I am I come … 54
    #97: Tell them I came, and no one answered … 55
    #78: I am the people—the mob … 56
    #106: Shiny record albums scattered over … 57
    #30: Somebody keeps track of how many times … 58
    #112: Thanks for the tree between me & a sniper's bullet … 59
    #51: If, when studying road atlases … 60

THE PROMPTS: AN INSTRUCTION MANUAL

    Step-by-Step … 64
    Prompt 1 - Syllabic Sunday (Sevens) … 65
    Prompt 2 - Metaphoric Monday … 66
    Prompt 3 - Wildcard Wednesday (Abecederian) … 67
    Prompt 4 - Wildcard Wednesday (Anaphora) … 68
    Prompt 5 - Wildcard Wednesday (Anaphora & Parallelism) … 69
    Prompt 6 - Wildcard Wednesday (Prose Poem) … 70
    Prompt 7 - Free Verse Friday … 71
    Prompt 8 - Free Verse Friday #2 (Ekphrastic Poem) … 72

SOURCE CODE: POEMS FROM INDIVIDUAL CONTRIBUTORS

C. G. Brown
NPR 75
Joel Dias-Porter
The Bukowski in You 76
Sharan Strange
The Child Who Cried in the Womb 79
Jonterri Gadson
Glossary of Selected Terms 80
Rupert Fike
Feedback 81
Jules Gibbs
Even the Corpse Wants to Be Beautiful 82
There's something about my slowness 82
Gabe Moses
Bruce Transitional Housing, 5:01 P.M. Any Given Weeknight 84
L. Lamar Wilson
Family Reunion, 1993 85
M. Ayodele Heath
Dusk of the Afrikaner 86
Hester L. Furey
Lunar Barque 88
Teri Elam
Call and Response: My Peoples 89

MISSION

"A book is made from a tree. It is an assemblage of flat, flexible parts (still called "leaves") imprinted with dark pigmented squiggles. One glance at it and you hear the voice of another person, perhaps someone dead for thousands of years. Across the millennia, the author is speaking, clearly and silently, inside your head, directly to you. Writing is perhaps the greatest of human inventions, binding together people, citizens of distant epochs, who never knew one another. Books break the shackles of time — proof that humans can work magic."

Carl Sagan, Cosmos

Introduction

Yona Harvey

You don't have to be "on Facebook" to enjoy the poems in *Electronic Corpse*. Sure, the poems were made with fleeting status updates and comment lines, but, don't be fooled—these verses are rooted in the communal creation processes of exquisite corpse and renga—perhaps, some of the first artistic social networks. M. Ayodele Heath has captured these once endangered poems and organized them with section headings. He has included also an instruction manual, independently written poems by contributors, notes, and contributor bios—the contents much like those of a print anthology. *Electronic Corpse* is unique, though, because it highlights the usefulness of online platforms for artistic communities; archives poems that would otherwise get lost in the digital hustle; and, in a time where much information on The Internet floats in an up-for-grabs manner without author credits, meticulously cites original source materials (poems, poets, lines of poetry), and grants contributors solo moments that showcase poets' voices away from the communal choir.

Poetry lovers and writers will appreciate the spontaneity and spark of these poems. The five sections of *Electronic Corpse* are organized as "The Consciousness," "Voice Lessons," "Love, COBOL, & Other Forgotten Languages," "Animation," and "I-Making & Mine-Making: A Paradox." The sections provide a framework, of course, but they also promote the idea that while hundreds of posts, updates, and news clips bounce about cyberspace, human beings can still push through the noise—and make art of it. In this case, Heath recognizes and catalogs spontaneous, playful patterns of theme, language, and homage. Thus, the reader experiences Heath's literary screenshot, the digitally assembled poems now held in place.

But within these poems, too, are tangents that lead to delight. A line never really "gets away," because there is always the next contributor, who meditates on it, and, with the addition of new words, reels it in. But if a line were to run, so what? Who would the reader "blame"? There's a whimsy and generosity inherent in the reader's interactions with these works. The poems belong to the group. And so the poems are not about perfection, but the wild observations, whit, and elation these poems contain. Reading *Electronic Corpse* is like watching a game of spades spun into verse. And by the end, the reader is eager to play. With the rules carefully explained, Heath gives readers this chance.

Within the sections, the poems are numbered and titled, and the collective authors attributed at the end of each work. The individual lines are not attributed, and that is part of the fun. The poems stand on their own while honoring the collective. These poems "break the shackles of time," just as Carl Sagan hinted. Now you see us, now you don't, they say in "#33: I've included this letter in the group":

So fling, as far as memory can throw

the red flowers, jewels, silks, incenses, wine—

a shrine to the We who might have been, the

empty shelf, dusty spiderweb singing,

Oh, come all ye faithful joyful and sparse.

We, priests of the invisible, await.

There's strength in numbers, the adage goes. And each poem soars with a strange, negotiated authority. And upon arrival at "I-Making & Mine-Making: A Paradox," the reader is prepared, has encountered lines by Anne Waldman, Jeffrey McDaniel, and Harryette Mullen—perhaps, without knowing. The reader may tuck the poems away for tomorrow or power up on social media and start a new round. Either way, satisfaction will follow.

Foreword
by Christina Springer

POETS FORM FRIENDSHIPS that span geography. Until the advent of social media, poets' sole methods of convening were through conferences, workshops, and readings. Typically, when they'd come together, poets would share favorite poems, critique each other's work and discuss new ideas. Much of our historical knowledge of these interpersonal aspects of poetry history comes from photographs, journals, and letters. In the digital era of disposable e-mails, instant-messages, and selfies—where websites, and even entire worlds come and go (remember GeoCities and myspace?)—the lives of artists, their relationships, and their artistic collaborations are not being archived.

Likewise, throughout history poets have been in artistic dialogue with each other. For example, W.H. Auden's "Musee des Beaux Arts," Muriel Rukeyeser's "Waiting for Icarus," and William Carlos Williams' "Landscape with the Fall of Icarus" commented on each other's poems and on Pieter Bruegel's painting, "Landscape with the Fall of Icarus." These poems span decades and never did the artists engage in direct dialogue. Using 21st century tools, we can continue this old age practice in a new way. Electronic Corpse: Poems from A Digital Salon documents an ephemeral and transitory artistic occurrence of collaborative poems created via social media.

As an original player of Electronic Corpse on M. Ayodele Heath's Facebook wall, I watched as time after time, month after month, truly interesting work was being created. I began to worry about these exercises getting lost. I began to focus on some method of preserving these very specific moments of poetry history in a format which was not dependent on ever-changing technology.

So, I asked Heath about his intentions. At that point, the primary intention was doing the work. Heath was making and holding a playful place for poets to creatively dialogue in a text-driven environment, which is increasingly encroached upon by cats and twerking videos. He was right. There is something joyful and free about these collaborative poems, which were created with no expectation of a tangible outcome.

However, Heath has facilitated a body of work which transports a century-old parlor game into the digital era, which deserves to be documented. And so, Exquisite Corpse—originally played in the wake of World War I, at an old house at 54 rue du Chateau in Paris, where each collaborator added words (or images) to a composition in sequence by following a rule—has become Electronic Corpse, played on a Facebook wall, assembling original lines of poetry, where each

Facebook friend—whether poet laureate, or mobile-phoned pedestrian—carries equal weight, contributing lines and making work that twists, that turns, that is alive.

Heath and I met thirteen years ago as competitors in The National Poetry Slam, a movement which also sought to democratize the poetry experience. But, our friendship was forever cemented on 9/11/01, when I invited him to Pittsburgh from Atlanta as a feature for the Sun Crumbs Performance Poetry Series. That pivotal day in American history, the show went on for the group of shell-shocked high school students for whom Heath performed. Our lesson was, no matter how great the void created by catastrophe, words have the ability to unite us. This anthology is simply the next step for two poets forging that mission into the digital world.

—Christina Springer

A Letter From The Editor
by M. Ayodele Heath

INSPIRED BY THE EARLY 20th century French surrealist parlor game, Exquisite Corpse, we embarked on a 21st-century experiment. On September 7, 2012, on my personal Facebook wall, I began hosting a space for collaborative, poetry-writing exercises which fellow-poet Christina Springer later described as a digital salon. The goal was simple: to leverage social media technology to see if my poet- and non-poet friends would engage with poetry (and each other) in a way that promoted greater appreciation of the reading and the writing of the art of verse.

The results were beyond anything I could have imagined. So, in true Facebook spirit, I've embarked on a labor of love to share with you what I consider the best-of these endeavors, these electronic corpses.

As of this printing, I've hosted over 160 digital salons, engaging poets of all experiences and geographies—from the curious bookkeeper with no aspiration of publication to Pushcart Prize winners and even two state poets laureate. Contributors to these salons span more than 20 states, 7 countries, and 5 continents. A given electronic corpse might be contemporaneously composed in south Bronx, South Carolina, South Korea, and South Africa.

I am thankful thankful thankful to Christina Springer for reinforcing to me the importance of archiving these exercises. Even as you read these words, electronic corpses are disappearing. During the process of editing this project, I made an unexpected discovery: When a Facebook user deletes his account, also is deleted all evidence of that user's history of Facebook contributions—every photo, every status update, every like, and every comment.

What this meant for Electronic Corpse is this: Let's say a particular exercise had 20 poetry lines (comments) when it was originally completed in 2012; if one of that exercise's contributors deleted his Facebook profile today, Facebook would remove every comment ever made by that user's profile. So, if that user had contributed three lines to the group poem, the poem would now show as seventeen lines. Those three lines would be forever lost.

In the grand scheme of the world's problems of disease, war, and famine, perhaps three lines of poetry are insignificant, but who knows who among Electronic Corpse's nearly 90 contributors may one day rise in the world of individual authorship to become a Nobel laureate. Fortunately, I had the wherewithal to manually archive and catalog each exercise via 20th century text documents and spreadsheets, for without these manual back-ups, even just two years after its beginning, producing this project would not even be possible.

At the end of this collection, the section, "The Prompts: an Instruction Manual," details step-by-step instructions for creating your very own electronic corpse. Through trial-and-error, we learned that some prompts work better for collaboration than others. Some results were train wrecks (e.g., attempting a prompt involving a rhyme scheme), while others were rocket rides to the stars. I encourage you, reader, to go out into the virtual world and host your own digital salons. Use the writing prompts as-is, use variations on them, or invent prompts of your own.

I envision these exercises being used to strengthen bodies of writers in community writing workshops and low-residency MFA programs, but also in communities of non-writers looking to bond on a different level—from AA members to cancer survivors. All it takes is a Facebook account and a couple of friends. I can't wait to view the body of your own Electronic Corpse.

What has been created here represents an exquisite experiment: What happens when juried, curated (dare I say, elitist?) Western art standards collide with the unregulated, populist 21st-century frontier of social media? It is a question which may invoke fear in the hearts of purists; but, on the edge of fear, within these pages, sizzles the charge of electricity.

I challenge you to do the following before encountering these electronic corpses:

- Deprogram: Undo your modern Western expectations of what a poem is, of what it should do, and of how it should do it.

- Reboot: Consider the Greek root of the word poem, as a "made thing."

- Play: Throughout the millennia, poems have taken myriad forms in traveling from mouth to page to monitor. Embark with us on a free-wheeling adventure of another path in poetry's continuous evolution.

As always, happy writing!

M. Ayodele Heath

14 January 2014

A NOTE ON EDITING: To maintain the integrity of the electronic corpses as they originally appeared on Facebook, I followed the following five ground rules as editor:

1. No lines (or words) were added (or deleted) from the poem.

2. No lines (or words) were rearranged in a different order than they originally appeared—i.e., all lines maintain their original sequence.

3. No line breaks were added (or deleted) from the poem

4. The first line of the poem serves as the title of the poem. (For longer first lines, the title becomes the first few words.)

5. The following minor modifications were allowed with the intention of capturing the spirit of the original piece, while ensuring a consistent presentation:

    - Correction of spelling errors and obvious typos

    - Addition of punctuation (commas, dashes, periods, etc.) and/or capitalization for improving readability

    - Addition of stanza breaks

I.
The Consciousnesses

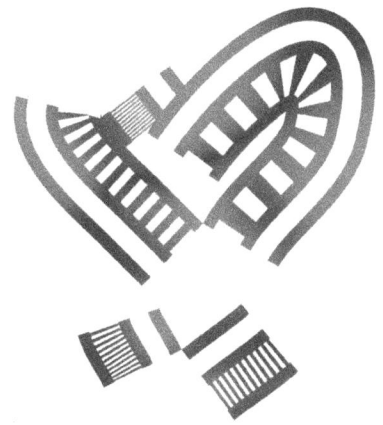

#67: We keep coming to this part

We keep coming to this part
this part where the distance gets thick
and the heat rises in waves, and each

wave moves between us like the thing we can't
voice. I form my mouth, but the syllables crash like
foam on rocks. They rise on air and

we appear to each other like vibrating vessels, or vacated skins,
or cherry blossoms gathering in the grass.
What once was sweet, now sours the tongue

fouls the long exhale,
but we keep returning, as smoke to lungs in a room ablaze.
We only know how to breathe it back in.

As we crawl along the floor, seeking cooler air
our mouths make demands: To taste the frenzy, the body's heat
the ohm between us.
Obliterating & regenerating, rocking endlessly, this blazing cradle—
The two of us in it. And nothing to save us.

Love, you are the hypertext of a white heat.
We follow where you lead us. Even as we burn.

Authors: *Joel Dias-Porter, Hester L. Furey, Jules Gibbs, M. Ayodele Heath*

#115: Japanese scientists unveiled a robot that plays the violin

Japanese scientists unveiled a robot that plays the violin. I thought, He looks much like my ex, eyes blank, mouth perpetually scowling, tinny sound serving in place of sincerity; the first one, a man-child of hollow shell with tinker toy knobs for brains, easily manipulated by electric impulses. Kneel, sit, stand. Not in supplication, but to ready, set, go away, chasing ghosts of girlfriends past.

The human violinists stood on either side, playing "The Devil's Trill" in a tight unison. In the key of John Henry's hammer. They didn't think about the small-hipped, brown girl in its grasp. The lineage of horsehairs slapping her belly. Or metal fingers on her throat. No. They were entranced by "The Devil Went Down to Kyoto," played in a robotic key.

The small-hipped, brown girl used the Vibrating Palm technique on the virtual virtuoso, sending the cleanroom into momentary epileptic shock. Tinny notes and gonging undertows dragging the spirits down, past Kyoto, past Georgians, into the maelstroms of memory, into the chaos that births new worlds.

And then he did the most magnificent, most transcendent thing imaginable. Like the one who walked on water, the robot waltzed the instrument of his desire across the floor. And even hands over ears could not keep out the echo of the small-hipped, brown girl's urgent voice trilling, "B diminished." One scientist said, "Our work is now done."

But his peers demanded a review, "Nothing of this experiment suggests it is repeatable! How does the human eye make water from this digital whine?"

Authors: *C. G. Brown, Rupert Fike, M. Ayodele Heath, Harley Hill, Kiom Marischiello, Erin Claridy, Christina Springer*

#19: This dream of water—what does it harbor

This dream of water—what does it harbor?
Slow ships on deep glass where movement surrenders

in a silent whirlpool, stuck, twisted as a wrung rag.
O' the colors that you bleed, wanderer

of the subconscious, sea spray, ocean's tumult, lapping
and the ship left at a cold canyon's depth.

As it turns out, water can burn
burn burn with the sizzling flame of cleansing.

This dream of water harbors a dream of fire,
flame-licked skin, cooling in an ocean breeze.

Singed coral. Dissolving island of smoke.
Ash and mist darken the melting pane of light

inside the sea–a boiling sea!
The laughing white gulls through the light wind.

Authors: Robin Bernat, Jules Gibbs, Jonterri Gadson, M. Ayodele Heath, Paula McLain, Robert Ricardo Reese, Jon Tribble, L. Lamar Wilson

#87: The five cool stars above this town

The five cool stars above this town look down
from their hill. They'd rather sleep, they are lost
knitted into our dark cloth of sky, light
bursting through at the seams.
No one seems to recall when they appeared, but
now they stay out of habit (or obligation) to sailors & drunks.

Once upon a time, they were a boy band
caught between harmonics & hormones,
their future fueled by delicate chemistry,
a powerful mixture of
testosterone, adrenaline, ambition, & heartache.

Spiraling into control, like a galaxy—
red dwarfs and supernovas, all the same to this town.
The five stars still seek the heart, exploding liquid lava light
through what is in the way.

In their stuttering light, a long, blue moan
splinters into iridescent shivers
as a one-time fan tightens her shawl. Turns the other way.

Authors: *Da Write Chick, Joel Dias-Porter, Teri Elam, Rupert Fike, Hester L. Furey, Jonterri Gadson, M Ayodele Heath, Jenn Monroe, S. Shaw*

#80: The winter her body no longer fit

The winter her body no longer fit, walking felt like swimming in blue jeans and a flannel shirt. She was a shadow, sporting skin. A dim light, blunted by darkness. A soft quake, aching to be felt.

When the white world whorled in through the suddenly opened portal before her, rather than shut the door, she lapped her tongue at the whirling wind & ice. Meticulously selecting each gusted crystal, she took platinum wire and beaded her heart until amulet.

It would not be long before she would stand, stilettoed on stages, lip-syncing for her life in a beaded gown, fashioned in the daydreams of the boy she once was. She then opened her mouth wider—eyes cold, yet inviting. Standing naked, baring porcelain breast, inviting adventure seekers to her mountains & valleys of unknowns.

She considered the word, reassignment. How her brain supplied continuity. Finally, she was grace. Was poise. Finally, she was home. Her body hers. Her life hers to share. So she sung. She found that the song had been her body all along. Each breast, a C-sharp; hidden candy, a whole-rest. She sashayed beyond her grave in the key of A-natural.

Notes rose and crumbled, harmonies wove themselves together, propelling her heavenwards. And so it was that she came to be the first of her race to live forever—a glittering name carried in the mouths of all future queens to come.

Authors: *Hester L. Furey, Rupert Fike, Jonterri Gadson, M. Ayodele Heath, S. Shaw, Christina Springer*

#55: They named me something French

They named me something French.

My tongue don't twist that way,

but my hips ululate

in fluent mother tongue,

speaking words never dreamed.

My Danse sauvage, a spell

Ca me donne le tournis.

Twirl twirl spin, a prayer

witness a world undone

by a Gallic spiral.

Je suis, tu es– il est

predella twixt these hips,

Banana skirt aswirl

African heart intact.

Authors: J. A. Brown, M. Ayodele Heath, Collin Kelley, Joy Kmt, Christina Springer, Dan Veach

#10: Once I pried open my doll's head

Once I pried open my doll's head

at the seam, hidden beneath her curls beside her ear,

and out fell all manner of things:

Her iambs, dactyls, her magical Negro blackness,

assorted raisins—some dried, some festering in the sun.

The box has always been a beautiful brown girl,

not always named Pandora.

Not all dolls are created equal.

This exceptional exception—

let us pose a question: If

acknowledging your emptiness means you're really full,

only voiding the void brings life. Only stretching open,

even if pried.

What lay beneath, left behind

was all in the poet's mind.

Authors: *Cherryl T. Cooley, Latorial Faison, Jonterri Gadson, M. Ayodele Heath, Kwoya Fagin, Christina Springer, Sharan Strange*

#105: If Kali were a car, what kind of car would she be

If Kali were a car, what kind of car would she be? Though all cars are Kali, meaning time, and death, surely she is embodied in one perfect machine, which already courses the black ribbons of our roads. She routes the magata, the dreamy state of the unfocused consciousness, the drive to the interior with its soft shoulders and wooden wheels, anarchy of roads like rivers that churn up boulders, disturb the bottom layers of quiet silt.

Even as the saline rivers appear to flow downhill, her chakras remind her the road is always rising. This is why her wheels are ever so sturdy while spinning truth on those lofty roads. But it's the rutted roads with their whump-bumps, that's why she keeps needing shocks. If the world is in need of constant repair, who is the master mechanic that will say that Kali can be made anew over and over again?

So one day, Jesus said, "Sweeeet! I could work with that confounding puzzle of horses, sparks and pump. Kali, lovely and dark manner of bride, are you the reward of my sufferings?"

And Kali transcribed the jive of Jesus' walk in maps, which looked like words, but which soared like psalms. The lines on the map were the black ribbons of roads before there were roads, where deer or hunters long ago had walked, which were the black words of her endless tongue.

Would you dare to decipher such language, feeling it strip you of sense, rather, and relishing in your renewed madness? Zooming into the horizon, hair aflame, at the velocity of a poetry engine's hallowed hum?

Authors: *Jennifer Balachandran, J. A. Brown, Rupert Fike, Jules Gibbs, M. Ayodele Heath, Richard Speel, Christina Springer, Sharan Strange, Darrian Wesley*

#143: When I heard the bombing

When I heard the bombing
I stood in silence trying to fathom the meaning of life.
Still, my rapidly beating heart could not

drown out the distant screams.
A giant strangeness bellows: why bother? Life is.

It is the twisting of the hand that holds the wheel.
It is the wheel of the sky that turns the hour.
It is the hand of the clock that breaks bodies.
It is the moment of reckoning.
My body is a crash site for mistakes, forgive me.

Life is a conflict and man is an expression of this conflict.
Bombs going off in my body exploding into
a double helix of yin & yang, of birth & destruction,

of fire & stone.

My own embedded armor, this shrapnel heart
aftershocked with desire
every beat a ripple extending out
into possibility.

Authors: Jenil A Dholakia, Jonterri Gadson, Monica Hand, M. Ayodele Heath, Gabe Moses, Mark States

#23: Luxury, then, is a way of

Luxury, then, is a way of
rendering wounds expendable.
Poverty, then, is how you make
the hungry heart crave what it needs,
although there is luxury, too:
Soft rain believes in abundance.

Luxury, then, is a way of
will transforming elements, well
upon well, until all that was
quivers at the brim, overflows
in a quiet spilling over.

Passion begins like this, a
drip-drip drip-drop to storm.
A hurricane inside a vein.

Authors: *Chard deNiord, Teri Elam, Jonterri Gadson, Jules Gibbs, M. Ayodele Heath, Metta Sama, Christina Springer*

II.

Voice Lessons

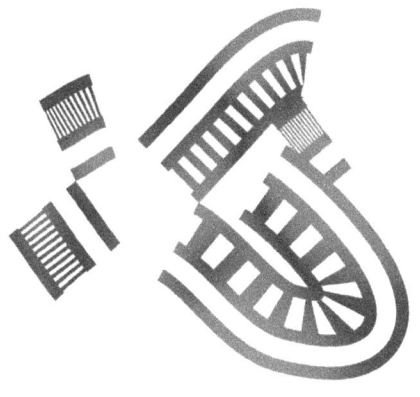

#57: The hardest part about

The hardest part about
getting out of a box
is choosing which hole breathes.
Fragile lungs, this side up,
yet my mind wanders

in circular patterns.
Squeeze through a beam of light.
Can foot fit here? Which hand
unpacks thought from storage?
I am an opening

in a cracked-tooth mouth. Laugh.
Spit. Till the cardboard's wet
& oozes down the side.
What first breaks through is voice—
silence out of its cage,

rage reborn from silence.
Stuttered song, stripped of sense,
strewn about the lea, bronzed.
The hard part is knowing
the true meaning of the song

Authors: *Cherryl T Cooley, Darnell Fine, Tracey Foxworth, Jonterri Gadson, M. Ayodele Heath, LaSada Lloyd Owens III, Rick Robinson, Sharan Strange, Candace G. Wiley, L. Lamar Wilson*

#33: I've included this letter in the group

I've included this letter in the group.
Invisible ink. Lemon, then fire

and, should its charred skin belie a language,
eat Romanesco broccoli to know,

then read the remains. Ash & smoke signals
are traveling, traveling, but never

rest. Unpurse the mouth. Let the coins in your eyes
pay postage for this message to hereafter.

So fling, as far as memory can throw
the red flowers, jewels, silks, incense, wine—

a shrine to the We who might have been, the
empty shelf, dusty spiderweb singing,

Oh come all ye faithful joyful and sparse.
We, priests of the invisible, await.

Authors: *Lori Desrosiers, Jennifer L. Freeman, M. Ayodele Heath, Metta Sama, Christina Springer*

#44: God of breathing

God of breathing,
God of scattering points of light, dying heat,
God of a thousand tongues, scattered across the Earth in a blizzard of blossoms & lusts & rain,
God of tippy toes tapping the hard wood of a broken morning,
God of my good leg and my other good leg,
God of fragmented bottles, of alley-cat operas, of home among the ashes,
God of mercy, whose last name is Help-Us-All.

God of unbelievers in yet another gorgeous dress,
God of yes,
God of barefoot races,
God of forgotten things—forgotten lovers, forgotten languages, forgotten recipes—lost and found again; forgotten soils, forgotten songs, forgotten ways home; forgotten sundresses in the backs of closets, forgotten secrets in the backs of journals, forgotten favorite colors becoming anew in the east each day at dawn.

God of mounting the stairs, limning the arc of cathedral shadows,
God of jokers, with his five aces,
God of oui, God of sí, God of na'am, God of tak, of ja, of bee-ni, of jouissance, of oh God
yes and yes and yes.

God of singing canary sunshine that casts the shadows of doubt among the bosoms of
earth,
God of all the goddesses, ochre-colored, lining hushed interior caves,
God of stillness, of quiet before torrent & chaos, of water that thirsts for hapless human
flesh,
God of darkness, gentle in its caress,
God of _____

God of shrieks and whistles, fugues and arias, thunderclaps and earthquakes, who created the world with sound,

God of too many names co-opted for too many wars,
God of The End—Alpha,
God of The Beginning—Omega,
God of midnight shhhhhhhhh, of mounting laughter of pleasure of pleasure oh God of pleasure!

Authors: C. G. Brown, Malia Carlos, Da Write Chick, Chard deNiord, Rupert Fike, Hester L. Furey, Jonterri Gadson, Jerri Hardesty, M. Ayodele Heath, Gabe Moses, Amy Pence, Metta Sama, Christina Springer, Sharan Strange, Candace G Wiley, L. Lamar Wilson

#1: The small dog barking at the darkness has something to say

The small dog barking at the darkness has something to say about the way we live.
For the dog that chases its tail will be dizzy.

Worshiping the Dog Star, the dancers' grass skirts are swirling comet tails.
The tails of the comet know what the dog knows about the darkness.

Darkness pads in on panther feet.
To lie six feet under is to speak no higher truth.

Truth speaks in multiples of three, therefore six brings the feet of higher panthers to the grave.
We speak phantom paws leaving poems in the dust.

Orion in the night sky beckons with his phantom hands to scions of the sun.
Grafted to phantom fruit, the sky knights only the worthy as suns and sons laugh.
Come!

The small, barking dog is proof of the god-laugh, a guffaw of the cosmic flaw.
Darkness is not flaw.

I am of the darkness. I shall sing the darkness.
A panther proud of black, singing the moon down.

We are of the darkness. We shall sing the darkness.
We dark, we paw, we hold trees and jungles. We lick our asses and still sing the moon down.

Authors: Chauncey Beaty, Jules Gibbs, M. Ayodele Heath, Issa M. Lewis, Christina Springer, Valerie Wallace

#135: In this country you may not

In this country you may not
say freedom, or speak loudly,
have an ambiguous look
or spin wildly on your head.
Decorum is law here.
Go against the grain. Yell loud,
tap-dance when meeting lovers
in the name of art, but what will you eat?

Tell too much to your children,
Write dynamite into hearts
to hearts which close themselves to
the voices of the most meek.
Free the fear beneath your tongue
spit it out, then drink freely.
In our country, yes, you may
drink deliberately of
insanity; may even
drink openly of the fire
in a public theater.

Loudly sing your liberty.
In the end, it's all you own.

Authors: *Teresa Doniger, M. Ayodele Heath, Harley Hill, Gillian Lee-Fong, Gabe Moses, April AP Smith, Darrian Wesley*

#53: One voice can change a room

> *"One voice can change a room, and if one voice can change a room, then it can change a city, and if it can change a city, it can change a state, and if it change a state, it can change a nation, and if it can change a nation, it can change the world."*
>
> —President Barack Obama

One voice can change a room,
One condom can save a month of worry,
One spider can bite a head off her mate to save the species,
One savior can candle the darkest future,
One Resplendent Quetzel can tremor a tunnel of angels.

One angel can mimic a gazillion quetzals,
One clown can point a hundred eyes upwards,
One man can terrorize a nation with two planes,
One prayer can lift a world with two hands,
One mathematician can prove a pin's heavenly weight.

One? Yes, & one struttin' woman can strike a crap-shootin' mob dumb,
One ring can rule a world, but only in a book,
One vowel can turn a man into moan,
One hand can turn a bad massage into a happy ending,
One line can bring the whole house down.

Authors: Chard DeNiord, Rupert Fike, Jules Gibbs, Jon Goode, M. Ayodele Heath, Christina Springer, L. Lamar Wilson

#69: Yesterday a man was sucked out of an airplane over the blue-tipped mountains

Yesterday a man was sucked out of an airplane over the blue-tipped mountains of Bolivia. He fell like a napkin swept from a table by a petulant child. When his lovechild was born, some fifty years ago to his mistress, Acotango erupted, covering the jungle in fire and ash. The villagers, in their little bowler hats, declared the volcano and baby to be one and the same.

And so for years, the man came to visit petulant Acotango, only under the blanket of night, offering papaya and starfruit, while his wife, Maya, scrubbed the floors of asylums. Meanwhile, little pieces of Bolivia were bitten away, commodities gobbled up, until its people gave Earth herself the right to be represented in court. It is said his wife turned
gray, and then to ash, in the act of chanting, while awaiting her day to see the judge. No amount of papaya could help her digest what she had swallowed.

As the elderly man, sucked from the plane, fell, villagers account that the mouth of Acotango, which had tasted so little sweetness, yawned at his approach. To him, life seemed quotidian, unworthy of such drama. The igneous face of his mistress burned him, even in his final breath. A metamorphosis that moved even his sedimentary soul.

Authors: *Joel Dias-Porter, Rupert Fike, Hester L. Furey, M. Ayodele Heath*

#75: A child said, what is the grass?

A child said, What is the grass?
Bouquet of blades clutched in her fist like an ice cream cone.
Counting, she reaches a number she doesn't yet know, and
deliberates a few blades with her mouth, for taste,
emits a bitter cry.
Fist unfurls. Grass falls. She learns to hate all that is
green and unexpected for a time until
healing begins, dreams
in green and growth, seeing sprouts in eyes, in tickling fingertips.

Journeys begin at the place where
keeping safe interferes with living.
Learning begins where
making paths through grass taller than the horizon is obligatory, not hellish.
Now, imagine the first cavechild emerging from too-tall green grass, crying, 'Wolf, wolf!' when,
overhead emerges shadow and act.

Poetry is made of this: the naming of that which
quietly requests redefinition,
racing full-speed ahead through the panic of phantom teeth, into the unknown,
streaming sparks like a Roman candle
till syllables illuminate, till line breaks burn, till
unions of contradiction and paradox fold into one another and rise,
vindicated in the face of bubble gum pundits.

What is the grass? the child asks, once more. But she finds the answer herself, where
Xanadu meets East Oakland, where
youth spreads its bare toes in the lush, green cool until
zenith becomes nadir, and truth becomes breathing.

Authors: Hester L. Furey, Jonterri Gadson, M. Ayodele Heath, Issa M. Lewis, S. Shaw

#63: "Man invented language to satisfy his deep need to complain."
— *Lily Tomlin*

Man invented language to satisfy his deep need to complain,
Man invented the abacus to satisfy his deep need to be counted on,
Man invented agriculture to be able to rise from the earth, again and again,
Man invented time to make a table out of it; to have something he can never have enough
of but still waste until he's out of it.

Man invented stories to create the lives he desires,
Man invented artisan soaps to cleanse himself after watching the Young & the Restless,
Man invented planes to satisfy his need to fly without wings,
Man invented yoga to get his entire head up his ass.

Man invented smoothies to satisfy his need to reap the benefit and do half the work,
Man invented management to satisfy his need to reap the benefit and do none of the work,
Man invented the cotton gin to satisfy his need to reap, to benefit, and to fire all his workers.

Man invented James Brown to tell us everything Man invented in "It's a Man's World,"
Man invented dance for feet to distract us from the problems at hand,
Man invented misogyny to rule by day, but forgot about the night.

Authors: C. G. Brown, Rupert Fike, Hester L. Furey, Jon Goode, Miss Haze, M. Ayodele Heath, Paige Hood

#61: Because I am a girl, no one knows my birthday

> *"I am like a tulip in the desert. I die before I open, and the waves of desert breeze blow my petals away... Because I am a girl, no one knows my birthday,"*
>
> —Meena Muska, from the article: Griswold, Eliza. New York Times. "Why Afghan Women Risk Death to Write Poetry." 27 April 2012.

Because I am a girl, no one knows my birthday,
Because I am a girl, I am every woman,
Because I am a girl, I carry the seed of Life,
Because I am a girl, I wait for the men to eat, then wait for the boys to eat, then wait for the cooks to eat, then I eat, as part of my training for womanhood,
Because I am a girl: nothing. The conditional clause is a construct of man.

Because I am a girl, I take less than I give; I was created to assist, guide, & love; the softer design from God above,
Because I am a girl, I devour life like a juicy peach,
Because I am a girl and I got skills, I am always the secret weapon on the court. I am a secret?

Because I am a girl, I am the support–A-, B-, C-, D-cup and all!
Because I am a girl, I unfurl the *be* from the *cause*, hurl the *free* from the *was*,
Because I am a girl, I will never stop hula-hooping,
Because I am a girl, I know that being a girl is hard work and being a boy is not all it's cracked up to be,
Because I am a girl, Beyonce is in charge of writing my anthems,
Because I am a girl, I know the stars are made of glitter,
Because I am a girl, I kiss my girlfriend in private,
Because I am a girl I exit the room with powerful grace.

Authors: *Candace Wiley, Da Write Chick, Jennifer L. Freeman, Hester L. Furey, Jules Gibbs, Ellyn Maybe, LaSada Lloyd Owens III*

III.
Love, Cobol,
& Other Forgotten Languages

#62: First, are you our sort of a person?

First, are you our sort of a person?
Trick question, so take your time, my dear.

Do you spiral inward or out, like
a snail shell, which has forgotten its

math homework? Dog slobber lover, rich
anticipation like Pavlov's dog? Type A, perhaps, with laser

drunk on sleep & funk, some worn slipper
losing itself under nameless beds

sprung on lovers' wails? Are you our sort
of woman, I mean. What's your thought on

silence as poison? Are you dying?
Wait. That question? Not a trick. Answer

As if I am the noseless Sphinx,
as if I'm the cat that's got your tongue.

Authors: *Chard deNiord, Jonterri Gadson, M. Ayodele Heath, Kiom Maraschiello, Christina Springer, L. Lamar Wilson*

#28: Everything measured. A man twists

Everything measured, a man twists
half a life into a poem,

the other half will never read
with eyes—yet with her fingertips,

he traces the aches of absence
as if he were her braille. Still,

touch is the language which does not
br – bre – ache – bre – break – brai— braille – br aide.

A language which the tongue can taste:
her skin—a hungry mouth waiting—

his skin—a half life, an open
book of flesh—decaying, for her

breath to rush through him. Like fresh blood.
Till he is living word. Or gone.

Authors: *Teri Elam, Rupert Fike, Hester L. Furey, Jonterri Gadson, M. Ayodele Heath, Metta Sama, Keith S. Wilson*

#43: Both of them were history, even before one

Both of them were history, even before one
was a number. Sometimes, almost subliminal,
we know the wholeness of zero, of nothingness, which
is the hole at the bottom of the sea. Or a woman's heart,
which was won, even before we were history
groomed perennially

to slowbloom—a reef hedging the shore of memory.

What cruel author would craft
a story with such fearsome hands? It reaches up

& yanks you back
when it opens a grimace. Step into the maw,

past its not-so-sharp teeth.
But when it closes, no one escapes, not even
the giggling fire with its wind-mussed hair, or her sister's tongues.

Authors: *Tara Betts, C. G. Brown, M. Ayodele Heath, Bianca Spriggs, Christina Springer, Frank X Walker, Keith S. Wilson*

#138: We married for acceptance: to stall the nagging

—after Carlos Barria's photograph of a couple waiting to take part in a mass, staged wedding in Shanghai.

We married for acceptance: to stall the nagging,
the persistent tongues rapping at our closed front door,
which would soon become our eyes.
Our apathy began before my dress was dragging.
Our hearts and minds constantly looking for
a different kind of love—not found in each other.
The blank expressions on our faces reflect
the emptiness in our souls,
reflect the dull glow of Android light, yearning connections where
none could be found between two humans sharing little more than
the room and the moment.

He, morning sunshine, me, spring wind
just desiring open meadows
of lotus blossoms—any thing not made of glass. Some thing
of skin, of teeth, of
bragging about the past,
dreaming of a future, any day not clothed in distances.

Oneness becomes unglued from our dry stares of indifference.
Before we ever come together, we fall apart.

Authors: *Lynn Alexander, Jennifer Balachandran, Teresa Doniger, Tracey Foxworth, M. Ayodele Heath, Gabe Moses, S. Shaw, Mark States*

#36: In an effort to get people to look into each other's eyes more

In an effort to get people to look into each other's eyes more, and also to appease the mutes, the government has decided to allot each person exactly one hundred and sixty-seven words per day. It is said that prime numbers summon the spirit of the Prime Mover, and, in so doing, repair our damaged connections. In this new economy of words, poets get rich peddling their alleged perfect systems for saying all you want to say in one day's time. In open windows above the bazaars, thieves' ears pan the rivers of streets, collecting dust of metaphors like gold.

The First, a terrorist group, brutally murdered The One in broad daylight, which caused her followers to also only speak 17 syllables twice daily and wear face coverings made from 17 tongues of animal flesh, like the ones they stitched to her face when they desecrated her body. In honor of her memory, cabals of beatniks gather in basements, poring over texts from the days when words were as reliable and ubiquitous as sunlight and translating meaning into 5/4 time melodies.

Now that eyes have learned to speak, the citizenry has realized that one hundred and sixty-seven words per day is a generous allotment, perhaps even too generous, possibly in gross excess of what should or must be said. No one says this out loud. They just look at each other and know it's true. Some people abused this power.

The Ancient, who tutored The One as a small child, fell over screaming one night, remembering how those who spoke with their eyes almost drove her to commit suicide during her Self-Smelling Time. In violation of her utterance allotment, she was sentenced to stoning after her tongue was cut out.

As the mutes are appeased by fewer chatting heads, more people become like them, meditating thru silent stares and primordial sounds, breathing more deeply, a more natural state like sand on a beach. Lethe group velocity waves: u (x, t) your ecstasy = A sin [amniotic sine], noise and velocity waves shatter invisible grain after eardrum, after helix-shifting hell.

So, silence then ripples and disperses gold for the thieves waiting behind purple curtains hiding the open windows above the bizarre. And after 167 utterances are spent, after reverberations become murmurs, become mum. After eyes unveil, at times too much, they close and prepare for the dream.

In The Dream, The Prime Mover, The First, The One, and The Ancient endure a sentence at the Round Table of Eternity, taking turns uttering one pained syllable per second, till their utterances are reduced to an argument of Tick and Tock. An argument which no one ever wins. An argument withering them to a chant in sand, forever and ever, Amen.

The Mother of The One knows this eternal sound: It is the chant of rippling labor, the hum of mournful lullabies, and the drone of 17 plus one plus one praying tongues, all calling forth The Dream. The dream deferred spiraling recklessly through perpetuity, clashing into 167 cacophonous moans, and birthing mutations of flashing eyelids.

Authors: C. G. Brown, Teri Elam, Jennifer L. Freeman, Jonterri Gadson, Jules Gibbs, M. Ayodele Heath, Christina Springer, Gloria Lawson Sylvester

#131: Above us, stars. Beneath us, constellations.
—after "Two Worlds" by Romare Bearden

Above us, stars. Beneath us, constellations
of uncertainties. Holding our feet,
the deep hatred that coiled cozily around my heart.
Till ash do us part, till dust do us
in, or swirling starlight crushes all death and rises rejoicing.

I witness the profound void within color & outside time.
With this ring, I reboot years—till hours become ours
and ours becomes mine, and minds meld together in one
infinite circle swirling around us.

The fire of love has mercilessly engulfed my entire body—
astral vows, a Morse code stuttering.
Mental somersaults & verbal acrobats take charge
as I fall from orbital to orbital.
Excess of sorrow laughs. Excess of joy weeps.

What is love, but blues, worrying strings of stars, till
you sweat. The knees wobble. The heart races
& the stomach crunches
while we lose time and time loses us
in infinity.

Authors: *Jenil A. Dholakia, Latorial Faison, Jonterri Gadson, M. Ayodele Heath, Harley Hill*

#12: The night is fractured and they shiver, blue, those stars, in the distance

The night is fractured and they shiver, blue, those stars, in the distance.
Fractured seashells stacked to become the lighthouse of our dreams.

The stars' lights are pilgrims, shivering from the cold trip begun before we breathed.
An ocean pilgrimage, solemn diapason, like a voice that murmurs love songs without stopping for breath.

Solemn & mysterious, your love's *veve*, washed from my heart's shore.
My love is broken like dark stars in the distant night and seashells beneath my soles.

His closed eyes seashells, revealing nothing. I grind sand between my teeth.
Was my love a tambourine of teeth, signifying nothing?

Once, I dreamed a love potion of sweet nothings drowning my heart.
The soothsayer's blue eyes whisper, The sea is deaf to your dreams.

The sea deaf, eternity deaf, my love you, too, are blind, deaf, silent dreaming.
My love is driftwood, bone white, silent dreaming.

Our love is a dream the sea remembers, salt-white and breaking, wave upon wave.
Dream with me and remember the taste of salt & sand, the waves of stars in a sea of sky.

We rub in our bellies one grinding grain of sand, one decorative star on a mistress's neck.
Belly to belly, we chant the sands into a castle of one.

Authors: *Rupert Fike, Jennifer L. Freeman, Hester L. Furey, M. Ayodele Heath, Gillian Lee-Fong, Issa M. Lewis, Colleen Payton, Candace G Wiley*

#125: Here am I floating

Here am I floating,
another year gone.
If I start to drift
beyond your reach, then
come with me, kiting.

I am horizon
improvising blues,
bending notes & time—
didgeridoo hues.
When wind says, *Go*, I
become its howling.

Angelheaded hipster
turns away, turns till
the turning of leaves
golds the grass with hurt's
colorful exit.

A day will come when
we perhaps forget
this all-knowing flight
into the blue light

Churning mysteries
of our stillborn dreams
into a haiku
that refuses to die.

Authors: *J. A. Brown, Bina Sarkar Ellis, Monica Hand, M. Ayodele Heath, Gabe Moses*

#133: Difficulties break some men but make others
—after "Stereoscope" by William Kentridge

Difficulties break some men but make others.
What kind of man am I?
A cloud walker, fog-lighting eyes—
not broken, but open; not stuck, standing
in a flood of tears. I float. I rise. I
swing back and forth in a tirade of bittersweet complaints
to be hanged by my string of disappointments, or
unraveled by the tendons
beneath a facade of accolades.

I'll be a man of teeth. Fists. A mind which grasps
mortality, embraces vitality, gulps down difficulties
which make other men break. But
the kind of man I am?
The question shrinks from me, lost in the reflection.
I hold two fistfuls of hope clenched tight in my pant pockets.

Authors: *Jonterri Gadson, M. Ayodele Heath, Harley Hill, Joy Kmt, Tanaya Thomas*

#3: The day came fat with an apple in its mouth

The day came fat with an apple in its mouth.
It was a Tuesday, and still I was full with Monday's cherries.

Monday was the pits; fortunately it was slathered in honey.
Honey, the end of the world is ripe with possibility,

but the ripe, unpicked, is soon a worm's world.
What does the early worm raise besides possibility?

But what is possibility without the noose of doubt?
Her body, an unpicked guitar, she is afraid of being bait for a loser.

The noose of her love sings as the strings of a guitar.
Without love, they are two spools, aching of phantom string.

Her love slithers away from him, readies itself for new skin.
Skin-tight, her dress is armor, fitting for a night.

Night is a battlefield where her love once lived.
Battle after battle, always the sheep, never the wolf.

With only the weapon of her own death daring the wolves,
who can delight in this rotted, fleshy fruit of her heart?

Authors: C. G. Brown, Chard deNiord, Rupert Fike, Jonterri Gadson, Karen Garrabrant, M. Ayodele Heath,
   L. Lamar Wilson

#17: I got news yesterday

I got news yesterday—
a teacup of fig wax,
waiting on a porch step
and a note attached, which
sighed, then bellowed pity

like wind caught in the trees,
moved on, became a song
an anthem, requiem
for hope (unlike Mozart's),
now whistling with the wind
again, now deafening.

I heard that you'd gone, spun
away, leaving behind
fragrance, a crystal dream
like the scent of fresh figs,
but your sweet taste, I miss
a kiss of summer musk
delivered by the breeze.

This air holds memory.
I caught it on my tongue
and I was love again,
feeling the sensation.
Your Carolina song:
Promises. Forgiveness.

Authors: *Robin Bernat, Cherryl T. Cooley, Teri Elam, Rupert Fike, Jennifer L. Freeman, Hester L. Furey, M. Ayodele Heath, Aisha Lumumba, Christina Springer, Gloria Lawson Sylvester*

#94: Like streetlights

Like streetlights
lightning bugs
wait for dusk
as children

snare last sun
in their teeth.
Mothers wait
on porches,
boards creaking
like crickets.
Fathers yawn
the sun down,
read the sports
hold their breath.

Goddess say,
Unhinged hearts
trump diamonds.
Doors ajar.
Peekaboos
uncover.
I'll show you
what you want,
like fireflies
simmering.

Authors: Rupert Fike, M. Ayodele Heath, Richard Speel, Christina Springer, L. Lamar Wilson, Karen Wurl

#139: If this life is all we have

If this life is all we have
why do we squander like pigs?
What is gained with mouths of dirt
wallowing in a sty of hurt?
This equator drawn between
poles, people, prices, and proof.
We should live Zeitgeist drunk, yet
we stack lives like hardbound books
that we have put off reading.
We separate so neatly.

Who will open the cover
and sit in a bay window,
read by the light of the washed?
They want to forget the dirt
the ancient germs on each page,
lively antidote to death
of the spirit. They will live
to die six billion deaths, but
no matter how many times:
Proofread, edit, and revise.

Authors: J. A. Brown, Teri Elam, Latorial Faison, Rupert Fike, Tracey Foxworth, Monica Hand, M. Ayodele Heath, Marie Ursuy, Robert E. Wood

IV.

Animation

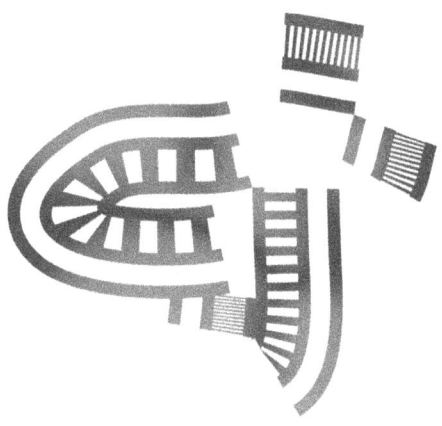

#60: We write to taste life twice – in the moment and in retrospect

We write to taste life twice—in the moment and in retrospect,
We write because mother tongue's been filled with lead & the erasure marks of colonialism,
We write because, after Reconstruction left us deconstructed, it's all we have left,
We write for those who cannot read—for one day they may see light in these verses,
We write for those on the #15 bus; for those who have been handed more eviction notices than books,
We write adinkra and hieroglyph for you must remember we are griots with a Sphinx nose.

We write what we don't talk about,
We write about what's under the surface, we write with our blood,
We right the amputated words, re-attach limber tongues tossed carelessly in landfills,
We write the wrongs we've seen and hope they don't come around again.
We write things that don't make sense, gestalts in dream language with one native speaker,
We write so far Inside that it becomes Outside—so when I sing, you recognize your spectral lines in the eclipse of the sun; so when you breathe, I recall the softness of the volcano's ash; so when you open your eyes, I, too, awaken & all the universe vibrates at the tenor of One.

We write graffiti on heaven's walls and God calls it clouds; our homes—new or liens—were bathed in art in New Orleans until some of us drowned,
We write till knuckles bleed, till time bends, till walls fall, till worlds end,
We write till mind reading is in vogue, again.

We write street slang & standard tongue and all between, ahead of time, driving censors mad with diaries & diatribes so that none forgets, so that none forgets, so that none forgets,
We write secrets to secrete viscous acidic solvents to evolve,
We write hushes into hallowed halls,
We write separ and etah to reverse the rapes to reverse the hate so that we can move forward evol(ve) with love.

Authors: Lisa Nanette Allender, C. G. Brown, Darnell Fine, Rupert Fike, Jon Goode,
M. Ayodele Heath, Christina Springer

#24: The trouble is, you can never take

The trouble is, you can never take
seriously, who you were yesterday. tomorrow.
Yesterday, a frozen river; tomorrow, a
rapid undercurrent, already in motion,
but with unseen direction,

sweeping things thought firm from under our feet,
urging us to go with the flow—or backstroke—
I can't even tell the difference. It's like when
you're taking a shortcut home, and the bridge moves

further into the horizon, shrinks as it disappears,
lifted by balloons, from a party you'd planned,
now an afterthought floating in the ether.
Somehow this makes my stiff, bone cage of body shake
with laughter. Imagine

when Never arrives on your doorstep, with its arms open.
You both know it can't stay.
Embracing it is awkward, anyway. Put the tea on,
and appreciate the grand absurdity of life, our attempts
to predict time's intentions.

Authors: *Teri Elam, Jerri Hardesty, M. Ayodele Heath, Gabe Moses*

#72: Ladies and gentlemen, ghosts and children of the state

Ladies and gentlemen, ghosts and children of the state,
lend me your fear.
The Gods, in their infinite insanity, have decided to pay attention.
This only happens once every millennium, so make it good.
Make trouble, make somebody happy, make some hoe cakes.
Life is but a vapor that appears, etches & vanisheth away,
eternal stability in what you do & say.

Make a baby smile coolly
at a flower flushed & breathless by the river's tickle.
Leave an indelible mark, not easily erased
like penciled-in notations
of a rough draft. Out. Damned. Spot.
Dick & Jane frolic in the killing poppy fields. Run. Spot.
The blue legs have guns & the Gods
laugh, but are not amused. "Show us something
to be judged! Every secret thing, good or evil; all
shall be accounted for, nothing unused!
nothing missing, nothing broken & what is this
that you have done with what I gave you?"
"Choose your words carefully," they say. "But let your actions
be loud."

Authors: *Rupert Fike, Jonterri Gadson, Miss Haze, M. Ayodele Heath, Kiom Maraschiello, LaSada Lloyd Owens III, Christina Springer, L. Lamar Wilson*

#93: These hands will never forget the prickling touch

These hands will never forget the prickling touch of barbed wire on border fences,
These hands are propellers tied to my wrists; some days nothing can still their motion,
These hands scoop up clouds, sharpen razors, & shave 5 o'clock shadows from sighing angels.

These hands have whipped me into submission, taken my measure, and found me wanting,
These hands cup your cheeks and remember when your ass was the same size and needed wiping,
These hands have held babies in Georgia and rifles in the Marine Corps, always aware that a life lay in their palms,
These hands are bridges bearing all the weight of my age,
These hands turn the page even when my heart fears what's next.

These hands have felt the brick and mortar of pyramids in Egypt, and the cotton and lash of overseers in Mississippi, and found the latter to be far heavier,
These hands keep time from heel to palm on cowhide drums till grooves evolve into fortune lines,
These hands have aged a lifetime; when you're on death's door, remember they contain a life line,
These hands are a rent party with 54 grinding, flexing individuals able to get over whether they are phalanges, carpals or metas (of the carpal gang).

These hands are payday and famine,
These hands are one part of my body I know G-d got right,
These hands make fists, pounding pavement till cracks break into breakbeats on Bronx blocks where b-boys pop,
O these hands these hands O!

These hands tell the greatest story ever told–wrinkle, palm, ache; callous, digit, scar,
These hands are feet; they run through hair; across voter registration forms; they run through time,
These hands rhyme poems for the deaf; re-write wrongs with the left; and fight for rights, making the world punch drunk on miracle wine; these hands, these hands; o these hands!

Authors: Robin Bernat, Joel Dias-Porter, Teri Elam, Rupert Fike, Jonterri Gadson, Lori Guarisco, M. Ayodele Heath, Sharan Strange

#32: Turns out the radiologist didn't know thing one about radios

Turns out the radiologist didn't know thing one about radios. His ex, Ray, was a DJ that knew nothing of radiology. Given this truth, we wondered how he selected songs that cut through you, that exposed bones like that. He worked the turntable like a surgeon.

The Radiologist turned the tables and dropped the beat on Ray. That old school boom bip, leaving him red, black and blue. Lipstick traces the edge of a black hole like a woman's mouth swallowing multiple suns—bap, bap, bap, boom boom. 110 beats creates more than two swallowed souls.

And so, one night while spinning in drag, Ray's glam world ended. Who could have predicted that the voices in his head were right? Who could've known that two tunes by Chaka Khan would prove so hard to blend?

Ray said, "I Feel for You" and wish you could "Tell Me Something Good." A host of indigo seraphim flapped peacock-colored wings, gyrated lasciviously on the diamond needle's tip, and sang out-of-tune razor melodies. This mix was like a slow drag with the preacher's kid. Ray's mix was—dub—dubdub—dub—Sunday night slow—dub—dubdub—dub—jam.

"Never again," the radiologist yelled at the pieces of stereo, "will you deny my special request!" But the angels sang on. Foolishness is particularly unholy, unforgivable, and always dampened by its own unpalatable particulates.

Authors: *C. G. Brown, Hester L. Furey, Jon Goode, M. Ayodele Heath, Metta Sama, Christina Springer, Mark States, Candace G Wiley*

#64: What if you knew you'd be the last

What if you knew you'd be the last
donut ever made? Would you tremble, crumbs dusting
your box bed?
Would you leave your sweet residue over everything
you touched—
open centers inviting pleasure?

What of the hole when you are gone? Would it, too,
be gone? Or would it remain
sugared in a roundabout way like
jelly-centered, chocolate, powdered, & pure glaze highs.?
Would you live the short age of a round life? Or the long hours
that make one hard and stale?
Could you ever love—living so much time with no edge, only
endlessly traversing the same brown skin?

What if you didn't know that you were the last?
Would you still embrace the hole in you
as your whole self? Or would you ache to seek
a most glorious glaze, a coat of
blind, bliss blankets—all pastries from beginning to end?
Or would you secretly hunger to be devoured? To know
the Wise Ones tell us our branches will never quite reach, not touch—
and believe this—this is the blessing.

Authors: *Kelli Allen, Da Write Chick, Joel Dias-Porter, Jonterri Gadson, M. Ayodele Heath, Candace G Wiley*

#130: When we grew up and went to school

When we grew up and went to school
we thought we might learn something new.
Not history's repeating bells,
but how a gun can't solve for X
and how a test can't fund a school.

Something more than a Scantron as
a way to understand ourselves.
So what's it really all about?
No. 2 lead poisoning?

Growing, spitting, dodging mortars
slipping through detectors and cracks—
not to weep, but to steel ourselves
against blood rivers across floors

Again. Stealing, as the only
way to add and multiply. I'm
one who understands getting by.

Authors: *Lea Banks, J. A. Brown, M. Ayodele Heath, Gabe Moses, Richard Speel, Robert E. Wood*

#41: I think it is interesting, though not exactly amusing

I think it is interesting, though not exactly amusing, how we go from day to day with no money. I laugh to keep from crying as my firstborn and last-notice both approach their due date. It's time we consider alternate forms of tender: pocket lint, loose strings, touch.

I think it's amusing and interesting how we listen to the those who make gun profits' views about gun laws like they're gun prophets. And sad that we've robbed ourselves of the memory in fingertips, once craving the touch of warm skin, now, the coolness of an Apple's screen or a trigger's slight pull.

I mean, at this point I'd take the precious metal tang of blood in my mouth from a punch to the jaw over this separation into rectangles. Although to be honest, her rubies weren't as red as I imagined. What we took for money—rubies, blood, the trigger's sensuous curve—finally failed us, abandoned us to a new calculus of longing—a calculus whose every addition left us with a long division, until there was no remainder. We couldn't carry the one, and we couldn't see the difference. And we are left broke and broken.

Authors: C. G. Brown, Joel Dias-Porter, Teri Elam, Jonterri Gadson, Jon Goode, M. Ayodele Heath, Sharan Strange

#66: A friend asks, "What was at stake for you in the Eighties?"

A friend asks, "What was at stake for you in the Eighties?" She's trying to figure out
Believable lies that make her sound worthy of
Cats, the 100 never-exiting visitors spewing hairball treasures and exploding flea eggs
Down Broadway theater aisles, screeching Andrew Lloyd Weber songs. Could the
saucy, red role of Bombalurina be hers, despite her
Endless, stuttering tongue and tangled feet that could only find
Freaked-out, drunk White folks on Cinco De Mayo leering, mole-stained lips
flapping silently staccato the word *pussy, pussy, pussy,* where
Going to the meatpacking district was like entering a subterranean, purple pleasure den? But that was the 80's when
Hot and heavy-handed men were called cats. No, that was her uncle's collection of
horn-playing, black-turtlenecked hobos. She doesn't remember what

Inspired her to answer the open call. It's as if
Jesus Christ Superstar and *Hair* screamed from theaters on every corner, and she was
stuck on a streetcar called desire, desperately wondering,
Khan… Chaka Khan, Chaka Khan… Was that a voice in her head? Or was it Melle Mel
on the radio rapping the opening bars of the red-headed lead singer from Rufus'
latest song? That's it! In her audition, she could
Love him and not know. How the Romans always came with whips, nails, palm
fronds. Hosanna hey sana, Chaka Khan, Barukh atah Adonai, Eloheinu, a salaam
alaikim, Chaka Ho, don't know how to love you behind the table in a dark theater,
Making love to the rhythm of boomboxes atop brave young men. Show her how to
carry music on her shoulders, bear it down through

Night that pin-pricks her with its cadence, its tantric drawl, its dervish rise and fall,
One of many standing on top of a pin, so powerful,
Purring themselves into Pygmalion transformation,
Quartered and halved—dragging through beats and steps to find the whole.

"Resurrection is not only the stuff of religion," she thought, "but also of art. Why
shouldn't I be the One to lead this iniquitous den of disciples to
Seventy-Third and Nowhere? To salvation, to peek under my clothing to find no one
There? Don't we all long to be seduced by illusions
Unmarried?" Voluptuous, wanton, xylose, young zealots abridge banality.
Verily, verily we say unto each other,

What was really at stake? Youth, dreams deferred yet to be dreamt? Our souls? Go ask
Alice when she's ten, nine, eight, seven
X-acto-knifing stars into black construction paper as a child.
You never truly know who is black, or
Zebra, leading a herd of cats out of the jungle, in song

Authors: Malia Carlos, M. Ayodele Heath, Kiom Maraschiello, Clela Reed, S. Shaw, Christina Springer

#126: Most animals can't

Most animals can't
talk, but this one can—
never heard by most,
ignored by many.
Teeth, broken mirrors.
Listen to the sounds,
weighted hair rising
eerie as white noise.

Anticipating
bear around that bend
keep bending logic
when a tree falls, and
no laughing reason
can resurrect it
until the beast speaks,
Hokko no renga.

Seven terrifies,
but songs sing through each
mouth. All rise—sun, wind,
hailing kings and queens,
resurrecting trees,
mud, matted fur, and

Blowing fire beneath
skin, till men believe
what eyes dare not see:
Critters, in the wild,
uttering silence
in awe of a world
on axis tilted.

Authors: *Yaya Brown, Latorial Faison, Joel Dias-Porter, Tiffany G. Jones, Christina Springer*

V.

I-Making & Mine-Making:

A Paradox

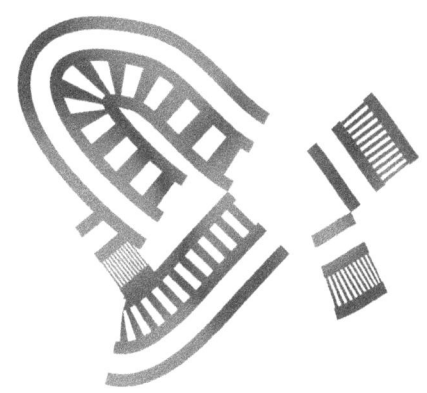

#141: A man is walking toward me

A man is walking toward me
but struggles to keep his balance on the swaying boat.
Catching his breath, he wobbles for a moment,
demons sweating through every pore,
eyes the blue of bewilderment, as if he
found Satan staring back at him in the morning mirror.

Grappling with the pull of his earthly fix,
he had only this moment to
indulge himself in the memory of reality, as next he
jumped in the swirling current to salvage
keepsakes—melodies and memories of his queen.
Lost treasures never float to the surface, they
make their way to the depths and settle into a sacred place.
Now it's me approaching him, wondering,
Oppressed, possessed, or simply otherness? What is he?

Parting the sea with my hands, I find the answer to each
question in numb flesh and still limbs sinking into new life:
Resurrection with no hope for hallelujah.
Scale and fin, we rise like five loaves of bread that feed
tomorrow's addictions, every one of them
unequal. We are broken miracles, beautiful
vessels on a meandering voyage to hereafter,
warning sailors of the alluring highs of rough seas, but

Xanthic tongues can't hold such truths and
yet the splitting winds reveal
zoos of night, open cages waiting occupancy.

Authors: J.A. Brown, Latorial Faison, Jonterri Gadson, M. Ayodele Heath, Aisha Lumumba, S. Shaw, April AP Smith, Mark States, Tanaya Thomas

#144: Just as I am I come

Just as I am I come
into this world of sin
and beautiful sunsets
ululating moonlight,
stealing joy in darkness,
forgetting I'm the salt
of the ocean, essence,
not Lot's wife. I spiral
syllables till I am
the glow of timelessness
pointing words toward you,
arrowing beyond truth.

Just as I am I come
to erect this house of
truth, respect, light and love,
bricks mortared with hurt, yet
forgiven for its nails.
Each shutter, every door,
leave them ever flung wide
for fallen and risen
to enter and receive
penance in its glass jar.

Like pain in a bubble,
my sins are translucent
and quickly replaced by
jubilant light, streaming
love, received, unyielding.
Consumed by love, not sin,
returned to the open,
I am just as I come.

Authors: Lea Banks, Teresa Doniger, Teri Elam, Latorial Faison, Rupert Fike, Tracey Foxworth, M. Ayodele Heath, Harley Hill, Aisha Lumumba

#97: Tell them I came, and no one answered

Tell them I came, and no one answered,
Tell them I told them, but no one believed,
Tell them I came, but I didn't enjoy it; the aftermath is always disappointing.

Tell them William Tell told telltale tales,
Tell them Teller told them to tell,
Tell them anything, the words are less than the message,
Tell them the stench of apples shriveling on the counter draws flies, and I am no longer afraid,
Tell them you are afraid, then jump anyway,
Tell them I love you.

Tell them I kissed and told, then sold the rights for a mini-series on Netflix,
Tell them every hard and ugly truth with no worry because they aren't listening,
Tell them we waited and waited, and then the cops asked for ID, so we left,
Tell them what they want to hear—or maybe not,
Tell them I am not opening the door; I no longer believe in doors; doors are so 20th century.

Tell them it's Veteran's Day and that my great grandfather's ghost in his dress blues and wheelchair wait by the front doors of the mall, demanding to be let in and sold forgiveness at a bargain price,
Tell them this is where I belong, my being is valid, my voice on record, and I am not going away; I will always be here, because I have always been here, right here,
Tell them to go away unless they have something that will improve the situation,
Tell them, the greatest story never told is the one you're holding inside of you.

Authors: Theresa Davis, Rupert Fike, Jonterri Gadson, Jon Goode, M. Ayodele Heath, Issa M. Lewis, Richard Speel, L. Lamar Wilson

#78: I am the people—the mob

I am the people—the mob—the crowd—the mass,
I am the red ant crawling across the clothes line,
I am the spigot even pliers won't loosen, rust-choked,
I am dark matter, unseen and only able to be inferred, but whose pull turns worlds,
I am polite and kind, so some people do not see my power,
I am sunflower, leaning into the jazz of night,
I am compost, steaming off stinks, feeding the worms, creating dirt,
I am the hem of God's skirt, star-stitched and eternally unraveling.

I am the infernal scraggle in Uncle Walt's beard,
I am the staircase guiding you toward near-death light,
I am Brooklyn Ferry, carrying generations in their thousands,
I am the wind turning days into nights into tomorrows,
I am aroma of Old World—jasmine & mudcloth, cowhide & chamomile, pheromone & myrrh,
I am complicit with the eucharist's whimper, a simmering mass, a crowded molecule's genuflection,
I am the reflection of star shine many light years lost,
I am the last and the first, bending into the 360 degrees of Self.

I am the middle—ignored—peg-legged chair waiting to weigh braying asses,
I am the furniture of the mind, where the soul comes to rest after a good day's work,
I am the clumsy, falling over for no reason, or maybe for a laugh,
I am somnolent kiss, wee-hour wending, noon-day peekaboo. Who are you?

I am—who is the nebula neuron? of where is the immaculate amoeba? and why is iridescent song?
I am the descent into mania and malignant memory,
I am otherwise and therefore, a rebellion of lava-flavored spit in the lover's imagination, reclining on the mind's chaise lounge, after,
I am the arising, the forging, the dissembling, the dispelling, the renewing,
I am here, where you find me now; there ,when you find me then, shining. Still.

Authors: *Chard deNiord, Joel Dias-Porter, Hester L. Furey, M. Ayodele Heath, Young T. Hughley, Jr., Christina Springer, Sharan Strange, L. Lamar Wilson*

#106: Shiny record albums scattered over

Shiny record albums scattered over
spinning terra firma,
my feet prepare to dance, but I hear no music in this place.
A brutal silence.

Revolving round & round, in a vinyl groove
lost. In space.
Thirty-three-and-a-third circuits each earthly minute.

A bright note emerges from the black static. Waxing.
A Dizzy B-flat, held to the death by ballooning
cheeks. Then, released.
I am born again.

Melodies cover me. A second skin
with you. It's like traveling Miles away
at the speed of brown spirits stirring,
bonded by one blooming note.

Authors: *C. G. Brown, Theresa Davis, Rupert Fike, Jeremy C Garland, M. Ayodele Heath, Joy Kmt, Sharan Strange, Richard Speel, April Wright*

#30: Somebody keeps track of how many times

Somebody keeps track of how many times
the man in the dusty room where they name streets sneezes.

Plenty of towns go down this way.
Whole worlds of them disappear from maps, their people
a flurry of dust, in a dark room, where light once
shone in a singular iridescence, dispelling all darkness,
for a time.

& for a time, those soon citizens held that black in their eyes—
that black, a coal to never hold the light of diamonds, but
able, if given a chance, and more likely, to heatedly
orange-blue entire families of nations with
fruit trees. Beer bottles. Heirloom axes.

They dance with ghosts on front porches marked
for demolition, swaying ancient bones to the rhythm of
one perfectly-round, mustard seed, banging against
an empty, white, plastic bottle. And
this is supposed to be enough—our dead skin
turning to dust, children
pallbearing our echoes into ever, down a street
whose name escapes

From fingers too wet to write them; in a place too dark
for dustmotes to be seen, let alone
gathered, reconstituted, remembered. When
time was a man who wound himself backward; when
wings flapping, branches snapping, water lapping the banks of
those tall, fatherly walls: The sneezing man,
the sojourn of his insignificance.

Authors: *Joel Dias-Porter, Hester L. Furey, Jonterri Gadson, Francine J Harris, M. Ayodele Heath, Gabe Moses, Metta Sama, Christina Springer*

#112: Thanks for the tree between me & a sniper's bullet

Thanks for the tree between me & a sniper's bullet,
Thanks for eyes, nerves, veins pulsing, for leaves,
Thanks for the panhandler whose eyes were clear,
Thanks for irises & wildflowers, screaming fire in the open field,
Thanks Moon, enormous Pearl; thanks Stars, bright Molecules in the high black seas.

Thanks, puddle frozen over, for my reflection masked in mud and leaves kept cold and unbroken,
Thanks to the silver blade of morning horizon for shearing off the bottom of night,
Thanks to mourning for burning away the rustling leaves in autumn light,
Thanks for imperfection,
Thanks for the winds of Art, turning us in so many directions,
Thanks for permutations,
Thanks grafted on spinal backs, hunched and hover or spun out wily as inverted rain,
Thanks for our afflictions.

Thanks means if you wanted to do it again, I'd let you,
Thanks means, my soul sees you and does not forget you,
Thanks for our humanness.

Thanks for chiaroscuro—that contrast that intensifies the light,
Thanks in flight from the backs of throats, till its notes arch the backs of fallen angels,
Thanks for compassion birthed from tribulation,
Thanks for birthing, and flying, seeing and wanting, grafting and hovering, turning and burning, shearing, screaming, spinning, hurting, for Life, for this, for Now.

Authors: Freada Dillon, Jonterri Gadson, Francine J Harris, M. Ayodele Heath, Harley Hill, Gabe Moses, Robert E. Wood

#51: If, when studying road atlases

If, when studying road atlases,
you close your eyes and point
to any crooked river, give it a new name, one with
the old power of the native language that's no longer spoken,
a river no one can spell but you

& should you ever bathe in such a river, in a future
which branches out like so many tributaries
stay where you are until the shallow deepens beneath you.
Swirl   fetal, in its wide mouth.

If, when you close the book, you find yourself
still friendless in the web of roads & rivers
spread before you,
unlock your heart & fly instead of
letting it move you   in the wrong direction—
albeit, with the right, unpronounceable name.

Roam: till eyes become rivers, till tongue becomes flight.

Authors: Lynn Alexander, Janet Barry, Chard deNiord, Joel Dias-Porter, Rupert Fike, Jonterri Gadson, M. Ayodele Heath, Richard Speel

The Prompts:

An Instruction Manual

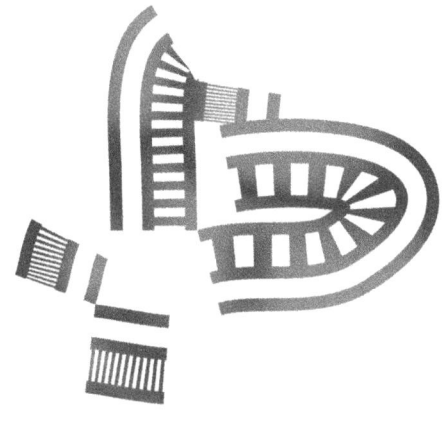

THE ELECTRONIC CORPSES IN THIS collection were created using Facebook, so all terminology in this manual is based on Facebook features such as *Status Update*, *News Feed*, *friends*, *tagging*, *commenting*, and *Privacy Settings*. This is not to say that an electronic corpse couldn't be created using alternate social media tools such as Google Plus or Myspace, but the instructions would need to be adapted for those platforms. Within this section, all Facebook-specific terms will be italicized.

The formula for hosting a successful digital salon to create an electronic corpse includes the following elements:

Writing Prompt: Providing an easy-to-follow writing prompt is essential. (The eight standard prompts which were used are included at the end of this section. Every poem in this collection is derived from one of these prompts (or a variation thereof.))

Tagging: *Tagging* users allows greater visibility of the exercise across Facebook and increases engagement. *Tagging* also allows some influence over the mix of poets and "non-poets." (As of this printing, Facebook only allows *tagging* ten *friends* in the initial *Status Update*.)

Privacy Settings: Setting *Privacy Settings* for the *Status Update* allows the host to control the pool of participants.

Line Count: Providing the line count within the prompt lets everyone know when the electronic corpse is finished, and allows writers to write in anticipation of an ending.

After the final line, I would post a hashtag symbol (#), to signal to everyone that the exercise is closed.

TIP: In order to allow easier tracking of the line numbers, it's essential to restrict the use of the *comments* section to only include lines contributing to the poem—i.e., the *comments* section should not be used for *tagging* additional people; also, users should not type extraneous *comments* such as "Nice line!" or "Is anybody out there?" until *after* the exercise is closed. Otherwise, tracking the number of lines becomes a nightmare, not only for the host, but for everyone playing along!

First line, or Stem Cell: To promote community-building and the reading of other authors, I triggered each electronic corpse with a first line, or stem cell, excerpted from an existing poem or song. Stem cell authors here ranged from William Butler Yeats to Sylvia Plath to David Bowie to Jessica Care Moore.

Collaboration: To ensure collaboration, I instructed contributors not to contribute consecutive lines to a given piece—i.e., a contributor is asked to wait until another contributor adds a line before contributing a subsequent line. Beyond that requirement, a given user could contribute as many lines as she would want.

Viewing of the Body: At the conclusion of each exercise, I would post the completed electronic corpse poem as a *comment*.

STEP-BY-STEP

Set Privacy: Set your Facebook *Privacy Settings* for the *Status Update* which will host the electronic corpse to either *Public* (for maximum engagement), *Friends* (to restrict participation to *friends, friends of friends*, etc.), or *Custom* (to restrict participation to a closed community to allow for a "curated" electronic corpse.)

Choose a Prompt: Select a prompt from the list of prompts which follow (or create your own).

Set-up the Prompt: Setting-up the prompt involves two steps—the writing prompt and the *tagging*—which are both done before you click, *Post*.

Type out the text of the prompt: In your *Status Update,* type the text of the prompt and make sure the prompt includes language about the line count, but don't click *Post* just yet!

Tag 10 friends for the exercise: Within the *Status Update,* following the text for the prompt, tag 10 *friends*. While the exercises are open to all, *tagging friends* is a way to ensure that the exercise gets noticed in all of the madness of your *friends' News Feeds*. For best results, mix it up and *tag friends* with different backgrounds and aesthetic sensibilities.

Post the prompt: Now, click *Post* on your *Status Update*, duh!

Post the First Line, or Stem Cell: Immediately after posting the *Status Update*, which contains your writing prompt and *tagged friends*, post the first *comment* which serves as the poem's triggering line, or stem cell. This counts as Line 1 of the electronic corpse. As the host, you will be responsible for checking in periodically to keep track of the line count.

Close the Exercise: Closing the exercise consists of three steps—posting the closing symbol, posting the completed electronic corpse, and posting the source of the stem cell.

Post the closing symbol as a comment: I used the hash tag (#) as a closing symbol, but whatever symbol you decide to use, just make sure it is consistent each time you play.

Post the completed electronic corpse as a comment: Within this *comment*, I'd do minor edits such as cleaning up typos, introducing suggested stanza breaks, standardizing capitalization, etc.

Post the source for the stem cell: I'd post a *comment* containing the author name, the poem/song title, and a hyperlink to the stem cell poem.

7. Pop a cork and celebrate: Pour yourself some virtual vino and post *comments* celebrating each other's collective creative genius!

Prompt 1

Syllabic Sunday (Sevens)

The rules:

1. I'm going to provide a ***7-syllable*** line from an existing work as a first line for a new poem.

2. This new poem we are composing will be <<<20>>> lines in length.

3. You can add a line in the comments section below to build this new poem.

4. Each line must have exactly ***7*** syllables

5. You can add more than one line, but you cannot add lines consecutively. (For example, if you add the 3rd line, you can't also add the 4th. Someone else has to take a turn before you can go again.)

6. Did I mention each line should have exactly ***7*** syllables?

7. Everyone is welcome to participate, happy writing!

Friend1, Friend2, Friend3, Friend4, Friend5, Friend6, Friend7, Friend8, Friend9, Friend10

Stem Cell: He jumped out of a window
Source of Stem Cell: Diane Wakoski's "The Story of Richard Maxfield"

Prompt 2

Metaphoric Monday

The rules:

1. I'm going to provide a beginning line, which contains a metaphor.

2. We are composing a new poem which will be **<<<16>>>** lines in length—each line containing a metaphor.

3. The line you add must contain 1 noun or 1 verb from the previous line. (For example, if the previous line was "Shall I compare thee to a summer day," you must include either the word "compare" or the word "day" in your line.

4. You do not need to make sense from line to line—you must only make sure your line riffs off of the previous line by carrying a noun or a verb AND by ensuring your line contains a new metaphor.

5. You cannot write consecutive lines—meaning, someone else has to add a line before you can add a line.

6. Happy writing!

Friend1, Friend2, Friend3, Friend4, Friend5, Friend6, Friend7, Friend8, Friend9, Friend10

Stem Cell: It's snowing in a way that reminds me of people who rarely complain

Source of Stem Cell: Ani Gjika's "Home"

Prompt 3

Wildcard Wednesday (Abecederian)

The rules:

1. I'm going to provide a line/excerpt from an existing poem as a 1st line for a new poem.

2. This new poem we are composing will be an ABECEDERIAN. Line 1 must begin with a word that starts with the letter "A"; line 2 must begin with a word that begins with the letter "B".... & line 26 must begin with a word that starts with the letter "Z."

3. You can add a line in the comments section below to build this abecedarian.

4. You can add more than one line, but you cannot add lines consecutively. (For example, if you add the 3rd line, you can't also add the 4th. Someone else has to take a turn before you can go again.)

5. Happy writing!

Friend1, Friend2, Friend3, Friend4, Friend5, Friend6, Friend7, Friend8, Friend9, Friend10

Stem Cell: All lovely things will have an ending

Source of Stem Cell: Conrad Aiken's "All Lovely Things"

Prompt 4

Wildcard Wednesday (Anaphora)

The rules:

1. I'm going to provide a line/excerpt from an existing poem as a 1st line for a new poem.

2. This new poem we are composing will use ANAPHORA, a repetition of a word/phrase at the beginning of successive clauses/verses. In this case, the word/phrase beginning each line will be 'This poem'.

3. You can add more than one line, but you cannot add lines consecutively. (For example, if you add the 3rd line, you can't also add the 4th. Someone else has to take a turn before you can go again.)

4. The poem will be **18** lines.

5. Happy writing!

Friend1, Friend2, Friend3, Friend4, Friend5, Friend6, Friend7, Friend8, Friend9, Friend10

Stem Cell: This poem has no poet.
Source of Stem Cell: Mutabaruka's "Dis Poem"

PROMPT 5

WILDCARD WEDNESDAY (ANAPHORA & PARALLELISM)

The rules:

1. I'm going to provide a line/excerpt from an existing work as a 1st line for a new poem.

2. This new poem we are composing will use: ANAPHORA, a repetition of a word/phrase at the beginning of successive clauses/verses, and PARALLELISM, similarity of structure in a pair of series of related words, phrases or clauses.

3. In this case the structure will copy the structure of 'I am not a painter. I am a poet.', OR 'I am not _____ . I am _____.' The 1st blank will be filled by a WORD or PHRASE, the 2nd blank will be filled by a WORD or PHRASE.

4. You can add more than one line, but you cannot add lines consecutively. (For example, if you add the 3rd line, you can't also add the 4th. Someone else has to take a turn before you can go again.)

5. The poem will be ***16*** lines.

6. Happy writing!

Friend1, Friend2, Friend3, Friend4, Friend5, Friend6, Friend7, Friend8, Friend9, Friend10

Stem Cell: I am not a painter. I am a poet.

Source of Stem Cell: Frank O' Hara's "Why I Am Not a Painter"

Prompt 6

Wildcard Wednesday (Prose Poem)

The rules:

1. I'm going to provide a sentence from an existing poem as a 1st sentence for a new poem.

2. This new poem's form will be a prose poem. (http://www.poets.org/viewmedia.php/prmMID/5787).

3. Since the fundamental unit of a prose poem is the sentence, your contributions will come in the form of a complete sentence, rather than a line. This means that whatever you contribute has to end with a period.

4. This prose poem will consist of ***10**** sentences.

5. You can add more than one sentence, but you cannot add sentences consecutively. (For example, if you add the 3rd sentence, you can't also add the 4th. Someone else has to take a turn before you can go again.)

6. I URGE YOU TO BE WILD AND IMAGINATIVE FROM ONE SENTENCE TO THE NEXT. PUSH THE NARRATIVE FORWARD!

7. Happy writing!

Friend1, Friend2, Friend3, Friend4, Friend5, Friend6, Friend7, Friend8, Friend9, Friend10

Stem Cell: A woman lights herself on fire again and again.

Source of Stem Cell: Nin Andrews' "The Fire"

Prompt 7

Free Verse Friday

The rules:

1. I'm going to provide a line/excerpt from an existing work as a first line for a new poem.

2. This new poem we are composing will be <<<14>>> lines in length.

3. You can add a line in the comments section below to build this new poem.

4. You can add more than one line, but you cannot add lines consecutively. (For example, if you add the 3rd line, you can't also add the 4th. Someone else has to take a turn before you can go again.)

5. Happy writing!

Friend1, Friend2, Friend3, Friend4, Friend5, Friend6, Friend7, Friend8, Friend9, Friend10

Stem Cell: In a country they'd not visited in years

Source of Stem Cell: Ross Gay's "In a Country They'd Not Visited in Years"

Prompt 8

Free Verse Friday #2 (Ekphrastic Poem)

The rules:

1. I'm going to provide a line/excerpt from an existing work as a first line for a new poem.

2. This new poem we are composing will be an EKPHRASTIC POEM, a vivid description of a scene or, more commonly, a work of art. (NOTE: I urge you to use your imagination and let it wander beyond the time-space frame of the scene.)

3. The triggering image for this poem can be found in a hyperlink in the first line.

4. This poem will be ***14*** lines in length.

5. You can add a line in the comments section below to build this new poem.

6. You can add more than one line, but you cannot add lines consecutively. (For example, if you add the 3rd line, you can't also add the 4th. Someone else has to take a turn before you can go again.)

7. ANYONE can participate.

8. Happy writing!

Friend1, Friend2, Friend3, Friend4, Friend5, Friend6, Friend7, Friend8, Friend9, Friend10

Stem Cell:	Above us, stars. Beneath us, constellations
Source of Stem Cell:	Ted Kooser's "Flying at Night"
Triggering image:	Romare Bearden's "Two Worlds"

Source Code:

Poems from Individual Contributors

C. G. Brown

NPR

Your modulated voices come crackling across
impossibly wide, IMAX-round horizons
reaching miles past outposts of modernity.
The city speaks too loudly for you.
All panic and death, Cassandra without songs.
But here, measured, regimented,
you speak soft words to match empty skies,
lit askance by cloud-thwarted sunlight
and fields that grow no food.

We're alike, you and I. At least,
you're what I'd like to be.
Something new every day at three,
awake before dawn to play your role across a stage
as wide and empty as my passenger seat.
From here to seventy, your sojourn with me
past snowy woods and sugar beets

makes the emptiness bearable.

Joel Dias-Porter

The Bukowski in You

When the last pile of chips
gets shipped the other way,
when your wallet gapes
like the mouth
of a two-coated man prone
on a park bench
what else is there to do
but stagger out and
return to the shadows
of an empty womb,
then curl up like
the last macaroni
stuck to a paper plate?
You sense even the women
cleaning under the tables
and dumping the trash's last odors
wouldn't sweep you
into their dusty pans.
The red deck, the blue deck,
the shuffle machine,
all make you feel
like the darkness under
the dealer's manicured nails,
his Rolex stopped to watch.
Damn. Damn. Damn.
Everything you touch stutters.
You can't remember
what singing sounded like
before the Ace of Hearts
punctured your last lung,
can't feel your buddy

tapping your shoulder
asking "How much you down"?
You remember the elevator
ride to your room,
39 floors of sunk stomach
before the white scowl
of a towel spread across
the bathroom floor.
Suppose you were nothing
but a hand towel
in a $49 motel?
Suppose you lived
to lick beads of brightness
from a working girl's back,
but all you had
was parched lips
and a swollen tongue?
That's why whiskey
clings to the bottle,
slight burn in the beginning,
then oak smooth and
polished as an expensive casket,
that's why when
the last card turns,
whatever you hear
sounds like a bullet.
More so if you dig
digging in moist earth.
Even more so, if
you're a not a gardener
or a man in a straw hat
wanding the beach for beeps.
You're addicted to
the dance of the Blue deck,

but also to the way
the Red deck parts like
a pair of painted lips.
You're addicted to
to knowing that even
a gypsy psychic
can't find your card first,
no matter how far she
follows a palm's
rugged grooves
like wood grain.
You're addicted to
knowing the cards love
no one
but the next hands
to hold them.
Is there anything sexier
than the way
desperation's dress
hugs her hips ?
Anything sexier than
putting it all-in and
having the moment
Morse code thru your veins?
That's why you return,
why you tease your chair
to the table's edge
and post a blind bet,
why you peel the corner
of your hole cards
like they're prosperity's
last pair
of good panties.

Sharan Strange
The Child Who Cried in the Womb

I imagine the setting suited her—a pliant container
accommodating her will, its membrane stretching
in perfect affirmation of her reach,
even the assorted sounds and the light filtering in
—yes, there was a kind of light—merging,
reverberating her own pulsing song.

But her beginning must have been uncertain,
a winter gestation—nature seeking closure,
erasure of another cycle. The frost a downy lining
for a final bed, the cold's stinging reminder
that the body is but vulnerable nerve, tenuous
flesh. Being a seed, she was expected,
like all seeds, to endure by turning,
first inward to fatten her own heart,
then outward to bloom in vegetable beatitude.

Yet conceived in such a time, she would inherit
the sorrows of that season, the void left by migrant birds,
the sadness of all those who cannot see past interrupted joy.
And into her peaceful estuary would come waves of discontent—
the daily worries of her would-be father, the drum-tide
of her would-be mother's fears—echoes
of that territory outside herself,
its airy vastness churning, buffeting....

The water soothed these discomforts, so she cried.

Perhaps then she pondered a permanent stay,
that way she needn't decipher the world beyond her boundaries,
its rules or who'd made them,
or navigate the errant paths they'd laid.
In the primordial privacy of her little house,
she had sovereignty. She had the leisure
of unhurried desire and idea.

Later, she would only vaguely remember having relinquished Paradise—
shedding the supple, snug gourd,
amniotic dream giving way to the quickening
of body, tongue, speech,
blossoming from her own tears.

Jonterri Gadson

Glossary of Selected Terms[*]

> *after Nin Andrews*

What is: *skin*,
if not a taut swaddle

loosening; *body*
if not a warm swaddle

cooling; *blood*
if not thread

in a swaddle
made of body; *horizons*

if not lines
where sky swaddles

Earth. See *father*;
stars, if not swaddled

matter emitting light. See *spirit*;
wind, if it does not trace

paths around bodies. See *blood*;
the *universe*, if not outermost

concentric circle. See *mother*;
a *kiss*, if not mouths pressed

into wet twists; *taste*
if not flavor swaddling

tongue; *father*
if not the option

to swaddle; *spirit*
if not the smallest unit

of the swaddled; *mother*
if not hips

swaddling womb. See *skin*.
See *body*. See *wind*. See *universe*. See *blood*.

---

[*]   Originally Appeared in PANK

Rupert Fike

Feedback[†]

As arguments at Shane's Hideaway go,
this one was civil, the after-work crowd
debating which guitarist had first formed
an actual note from feedback, raw sound—
who had done it, tamed what's infinite,
the Jeff Beck champions up by the taps
taking on two Dick Dale dudes by the limes,
until barmaid Missy from Sussex,
she of the half-shaved head and tongue stud,
declared us all, *proper wankers,* for not knowing
it was George Harrison, his lead-in buzz-whine
to *I Feel Fine* (an F#, she said) in 1965.

We were all pretty much afraid of Missy
so we pointed for another round
and kept it to ourselves that, wait, no,
it must have been Les Paul who more or less
invented the electric guitar.
Surely Les, early on, down in his basement,
was twisting knobs, messing around as usual,
the volume a bit cranked, the amp too close,
and here it came, Pluto's underworld wail,
sine waves chasing their electron tails,
Les taking two quick steps back – there!
a sonic G, unmistakably a note,
all while Fermi pulled graphite rods from a core,
while Pollock dripped in two dimensions
this new world in a grain of sand, silicone,
what could be baked, sliced so thin, charged . . .
Les unaware, smiling at what he'd wrought,
Mary Ford yelling down the stairs again,

"Honey, please! You know that scares the cats."

---
† Originally appeared in Lotus Buffet (Brick Road PoetryPress)

Jules Gibbs

Even the Corpse Wants to Be Beautiful

There's something about my slowness

I'm trying to know, why I cease to divide

and begin, how clustered bones form no limbs, piled

into my own little slew.

Something more must live in the wake of the mind,

which is still something, still a mind, even

in the after, as something new that gathers

in the body's honeycomb, steeves in the hull

where protons unmake their pact.

I want a congregation of ants to sing a hymn,

a holy beak to dip in. A little lizard

to eulogize the grume, pale to my skin.

At my finer edges, decay occurs

most rapidly — the hinge from which

I used to jaw, the sockets where I waved

goodbye. Now all my thoughts are groomed

in the tongue to die. Two girls walk by.

One girl says to the other: *After one semester*

we still know so much less than the crows.

What the crows know is how to be alone

in the throat.   I try.

I toil, curl and crack against corrosives —furl

towards the place where I still shine. I shine

less. I miss all the sing and squawk, the talk

of talk. I could tell you how the wind swept in

and I was spilled, laid out, flat on my back—

tenacious burr, tuft of fur, a clot that clabbers.

I could tell you once these feathers were really something

in the sun, but you know it's a death march

even for the best of us, the tune

always goes: *da-dum, da-dum, da-dum—*

Gabe Moses

Bruce Transitional Housing, 5:01 P.M. Any Given Weeknight

When the social workers and administrators
and substance-abuse counselors have left for the night,
gone home to cook dinner
and shower us off their skin,
the place becomes ours.

We smoke cigarettes out the windows.
We pour the contents of smuggled flasks
into the WIC grape juice from the communal kitchen.
We face ghetto-blasters to the halls,
fill them with the tinny crackle
of hip-hop or country-western.

The old men at the ends of the halls play the blues,
and that's when you realize rap and country
are just prickly-elbowed siblings
with the same father.
They all speak hardship in different accents.

Little kids in sock-feet dance
and slide on the floors;
couples sneak the kisses they'd save
for their own living rooms,
if they had them.

When the iron-gated doors swing shut
and for twelve hours we're nobody's problem
but our own,
for a moment we dare
to make ourselves at
Home.

L. Lamar Wilson

Family Reunion, 1993‡

> *"When I am asked whose tears these are, I always blame the moon."*
> —Lucille Clifton

I give my cousin my hand & think
of the year before, how he'd held me aloft

with his, bicep pulsing against the weight
of my bones & adoration. *Can I get it*

by touching him? I wonder but don't speak,
don't let go until his slick flesh kisses

the commode, then trace curlicues & stars
into my stucco canvas amid his grunts & sighs,

stare at the moon I've made there as full of itself
as the one that had shone on us at the reunion,

our mothers in orbit around us in their own groove
with Frankie Beverly. *I'm flying!* I had beamed

at myself, gilded in his tooth: the only
shimmering thing in this dark, damp silence.

---

‡ Originally appeared in African-American Review

M. Ayodele Heath

Dusk of the Afrikaner[§]

> *Aku'langa latshona lingenanduba.*
> —*Zulu proverb*

I.

ONCE UPON A TIME, WHEN TIME was measured in the length of shadows, I met a woman—on a dirt road much like this one—who did not know the smell of rain.

How sad, she said to no one. *I want to know it.*

Her long Zulu eyes were not nearly as long as her gaze, on this day, impossibly February: heat billowing in waves; the once-White sun finally lowering among the aloes, by great pallbearers of Light, into the ground.

On the day I met this *umfazi*, I stumbled over her shadow & felt a sudden chill. Sure & black as thunderclouds.

Far beyond the townships, beyond rivers of dust with no memory of the sea, her gathering shadow was easily the longest I'd ever seen. It must have been the longest in the world.

As a desert without clouds, she said. *As a sleep without dreams.*

Such a shadow must have meant she was very old. Perhaps, the oldest woman in the world.

But I am not, she said, burning the pages in my eyes.

II.

THEN, LIKE A MIGHTY black river of Night, the *umfazi's* shadow fell across the Earth, crushing the aloes & the hills & the trees. & all throughout Zululand, the blackest nightmare of one became the other's dream.

& the sky wept.

[§] Originally appeared in *diode*

Like one who has not wept for centuries might weep, she said. *With the kind of weeping which feels like thunder, which makes the earth shudder, which portends the end of days.*

& some ran for shelter. & some ran for the sea. But millions more had waited lifetimes for this storm. Through moon, through sun, they clutched the aching earth.

Till rain & mud, she said, *turned tears & blood.*

& there they stood. As ones who have not stood for centuries might stand. *As if standing for something,* she said. As if suddenly aware of the straightness of their own posture.

Then they raised their faces like black moonflowers till the whole of Zululand was ablaze with Midnight

& stars rained from her tongue—this witness, this poet—so moved she was by their forgotten beauty.

Hester L. Furey

Lunar Barque

Sometimes in the morning

it's still there, rocking at the edge

of sleep. You could step back into it,

if you want, just close your eyes

and return to whatever

world you came from,

leave the aged body

with its aching hip and allergies,

the troll who stood so obstinately

in your path down to the water

the night before,

just leave the bastard there,

now its guard is down,

for the cats to play hopscotch across.

Its masters, the jealous gods of daylight,

have not got you yet.

The boatmen wait patiently.

You are free.

Teri Elam

Call and Response: My Peoples

my memory of ancestors rages and bleeds.

my peoples neither break bread nor drink red wine on sunday.

my memory of ancestors, a ragged gash christened in salted sweat.

my peoples do not heal.

my memory of ancestors blisters turned-up palms.

my peoples can not hold.

my memory of ancestors, a blood-stained millstone.

my peoples can not carry.

my memory of ancestors fat-stitches keloids into patchwork-stars.

my peoples do enfold.

my memory of ancestors, a faint forbidden prayer.

my peoples scream Amen.

Amen.

Amen.

Notes

The first line of each *Electronic Corpse* poem is taken from an existing work by another author. Consider this the poem's *stem cell*. The format of these *stem cell* listings is:

Poem Number. "Poem/Song Title" by Author

1. "Lighthead's Guide to the Galaxy" by Terrance Hayes

3. "Animals" by Frank O'Hara

10. "Natural Occurrences" by Sharan Strange

12. "I Can Write the Saddest Lines" by Pablo Neruda translated by A.S. Kline

17. "Arroz Poetica" by Aracelis Girmay

19. "I See Chile in My Rearview Mirror" by Aracelis Girmay

23. "Political Poem" by Amiri Baraka

24. "The Gardenia" by Cornelius Eady

28. "At the End of Life, a Secret" by Reginald Dwayne-Betts

30. "Innings " by C.K. Williams

32. "Gnosis" by Theodore Worozbyt

33. "Instructions to Be Left Behind" by Marvin Bell

36. "The Quiet World" by Jeffrey McDaniel

41. "January in Detroit or Search for Tomorrow Starring Ken and Ann" by Ken Mikolowski

43. "One-Third of 180 Grams of Lead" by Frank X Walker"

44. "Of Spirit" by Joan Larkin

51. "Domestic" by Carl Philips

53. "One voice can change a room" [quote] by President Barack Obama

55. "The Missing Project: Pieces of the D" by Jessica Care Moore

57. "A Guide for Black and White Crossing" by Katy Richey

60. "We Write to Taste Life Twice" from The Diary of Anaïs Nin, Vol. 5

61. Griswold, Eliza. "Why Afghan Women Risk Death to Write Poetry." *New York Times*. 27 April 2012.

62. "The Applicant" by Sylvia Plath

63. "Man invented language to satisfy his deep need to complain." [quote] by Lily Tomlin.

64. "If You Only Knew" by Ellen Bass

66. "The Eighties" by Brenda Hillman

67. "Heroics" by Julia Alvarez

69. "After the Weather" by Mary A Koncel

72. "Lighthead's Guide to the Galaxy" by Terrance Hayes

75. "A child said, what is the grass" by Walt Whitman

78. "I am the people—the mob" by Carl Sandburg

80. "Adolescence" by Nin Andrews

87. "The Poem with Wisteria Growing Along Its Margin" by Gerry LaFemina

93. "These Hands" by Makhosazana Xaba

94. "Traveling" by Malena Mörling

97. "The Listeners" by Walter DeLa Mare

105. "Alphabet of Mother Language" by Anne Waldman

106. "As You Leave Me" by Etheridge Knight

112. "Thanks" by Yusef Komunyakaa

115. "Japanese Scientists" by Richard Garcia

125. "Space Oddity" by David Bowie

130. "Another Brick in the Wall" by Pink Floyd

131. "Flying at Night" by Ted Kooser

133. excerpt from a Nelson Mandela letter to wife, Winnie Mandela, from Robben Island, February 1975

135. "Small Passing" by Ingrid de Kok

138. "My Second Marriage to My First Husband" by Alice Fulton

139. "If This Life is All We Have" by Dennis Brutus

141. "The Fifth Dream: Bullets and Deserts and Borders" by Benjamin Alire Sáenz

143. "Quotidian Poem" by Patricia Fargnoli

144. "Muse & Drudge [just as I am I come]" by Harryette Mullen

Contributors

LYNN ALEXANDER is Managing Editor of the *Atlanta Review* and tutors English writing at Georgia Perimeter College in Clarkston, Georgia. She is former editor of Poetry Atlanta, and is author of the chapbook, *Hanging Clothes at Midnight*. Her upcoming chapbook, *Man Done Gone*, will soon be available by Finishing Line Press. Her memoir, *The Indelicate Flower*, will be released in late 2014. She lives in Pine Lake, Georgia, with her Lhasa Apso, Randall.
Appears in poem nos.: 51, 138

KELLI ALLEN's work has appeared in numerous journals and anthologies in the US and internationally. She served as Managing Editor of *Natural Bridge* and holds an MFA from the University of Missouri. She is currently a Professor of English and Creative Writing at Lindenwood University in St. Charles, Missouri. Allen gives readings and teaches workshops throughout the US. Her full-length poetry collection, *Otherwise, Soft White Ash*, arrived from John Gosslee Books (2012) and was nominated for the Pulitzer Prize.
Appears in poem no.: 64

LISA NANETTE ALLENDER earned her BA in Theatre Arts, Performance, from the University of South Florida. As an actress represented by the Jana Van Dyke Agency, she appeared in the 2011 feature film, *Unspoken Words*. As a writer, she has been published in numerous anthologies, and online. Follow her on Facebook, on her blog at www.lisananetteallender.blogspot.com, and on Twitter @lisaallender.
Appears in poem no.: 60

JENNIFER BALACHANDRAN lives in Decatur, GA, with her two daughters. Prior to moving to Georgia, she lived only in states which border Canada, but being in the South has grown on her. She has poetry in *Flycatcher*, and work forthcoming in *Terminus*. She also posts her own poems regularly on her blog at www.flindermouse.com.
Appears in poem nos.: 105, 138

JANET BARRY is a New Hampshire musician and poet with works in numerous journals and anthologies, most recently *Looseleaf Tea, Two Hawks Quarterly, Edge,* and *The Fourth River*. She serves yearly as a judge for Poetry Out Loud, and serves as second editor for *Naugatuck River Review*. Janet has received several Pushcart and a Best of the Net nominations. She hold degrees in organ performance and poetry.
Appears in poem no.: 51

LEA BANKS, the author of the chapbook, *All of Me,* (Booksmyth Press, 2008) lives in western Massachusetts. She is the Poetry Coordinator for the Brattleboro Literary Festival in VT, and founder of the Collected Poets Series in MA. Banks has published in several journals including *Big River Poetry Review, Poetry Northwest, Slipstream, Diner, Sweet,* and *American Poetry Journal,* and recently was a fellow at the Vermont Studio Center.
Appears in poem no.: 130, 144

A two-time Women of the World Poetry Slam finalist, **CHAUNCEY BEATY** has been ranked as high as the 3rd best female slam poet in the world. Featured on TV One's "Verses and Flow," she is founder of the Annual Women's Poetry and Performance Retreat and the READY Woman Retreat. A proud ambassador for the Greater Than AIDS campaign, she earned a BA from Winthrop University in Psychology and an MA in African-American and African Studies from The Ohio State University. She is a native of Greenville, South Carolina.
Appears in poem no.: 1

Robin Bernat is an experimental filmmaker and poet whose work explores beauty and feeling and their provisional qualities. Her work appeared in the 2000 Whitney Biennial of the Whitney Museum of American Art; she has exhibited her work nationally at the Kemper Museum of Art, the Cheekwood Museum, the Masur Museum and the Museum of Contemporary Art of Georgia (MOCA-GA). She is the owner and curator of {Poem88}, a gallery for contemporary art, in Atlanta, Georgia, where she resides with her partner, Jon, and two cats.
Appears in poem nos.: 17, 19, 93

Tara Betts is the author of *Arc & Hue* and the chapbook/libretto, *THE GREATEST!: A Tribute to Muhammad Ali*. Tara is a PhD candidate at Binghamton University. Her poetry and prose have appeared in journals, anthologies, and multimedia projects. Currently, she works with the Binghamton Poetry Project, serves as a Poetry Editor for *Blackberry*, and curates readings in upstate New York. She calls the Illinois locales of Chicago and Kankakee home.
Appears in poem no.: 43

C. G. Brown doesn't write enough poetry, or make enough music. He does, however, probably write enough lines of software code in his day job as an entrepreneur and software engineer, and sometimes plays enough music here and there as a DJ in Atlanta's local music spots. C. G. lives in Atlanta, Georgia.
Appears in poem nos.: 3, 32, 36, 41, 43, 44, 60, 63, 106, 115

J. A. Brown relocated from Newark, NJ, to Atlanta, GA, in 1996, and began writing poetry two years later. He currently makes a living working at a local food co-op. Brown also is a freelance musician, performing with various local Atlanta acts.
Appears in poem nos.: 55, 105, 125, 126, 130, 139

Malia Carlos lives in Sewanee, TN, where she teaches English at St. Andrew's-Sewanee School and Chattanooga State. She attended Tufts University, Umass-Amherst, and New England College. She loves her three wise children, her two sweet dogs, and one good man.
Appears in poem nos.: 44, 66

Da Write Chick is a poet, writer, blogger, and publisher. She is the founder and publisher of *B Epic Magazine*, an online and print magazine and an enterprise with a goal to deliver ideas that inspire, uplift and encourage positive change. She also has works published in *Rolling Out* magazine and participates in various community service projects in Atlanta, GA.
Appears in poem nos.: 44, 61, 64, 87

Erin Claridy (Erin C Poetry to her Facebook companions) is a Miami, Florida, born educator who currently lives and teaches in the metro Atlanta area. She has been an active writer and performer in spoken word poetry communities since college and strives to use words as a means of enlightenment and education.
Appears in poem no.: 115

Cherryl T. Cooley is a Raleigh, North Carolina-based poet, playwright and fiber artist. She has published three poetry collections, *Utterance: A Museology of Kin* (2002), *Chops* (Nexus Press, 2004) and *Exquisite Heats* (Salt Publishing, 2008). Her work has appeared in *Poetry, Essence,* and numerous anthologies and literary magazines. A southern food enthusiast, she is married to a chef and formerly published poetry as Cherryl Floyd-Miller.
Appears in poem nos.: 10, 17, 57

THERESA DAVIS is one of Atlanta's best known performance poets, winning poetry slams and featuring at spoken word venues around Atlanta and the nation, as well as leading writing and performance workshops and headlining conferences across the southeast. She is a member of The Word Diversity Collective/Art Amok and represented Atlanta as a member of the 2006 - 2011 Art Amok Slam Team. In March of 2011 Theresa was ranked #1 female slam poet in the world as the winner of the Women of the World Poetry Slam.
Appears in poem nos.: 97, 106

CHARD DENIORD earned a BA in religious studies from Lynchburg College, a Masters of Divinity from Yale Divinity School, and an MFA from the Iowa Writers' Workshop. Co-founder of the New England College MFA program in Poetry, he is author of the poetry collections *Asleep in the Fire* (1990), *Sharp Golden Thorn* (2003), *Night Mowing* (2005), and *The Double Truth* (2011). Recipient of a Pushcart Prize, his poems appear in the anthologies *Best American Poetry* (1999), *Best of the Prose Poem* (2000), and *American Religious Poems* (2006). A teacher at Providence College in Providence, Rhode Island, he lives in Putney, Vermont
Appears in poem nos.: 3, 23, 44, 51, 53, 62, 78

LORI DESROSIERS' first full-length book of poetry, *The Philosopher's Daughter*, was published by Salmon Poetry in 2013. Her poems have appeared in *New Millenium Review, Contemporary American Voices, BigCityLit, Concise Delights, Blue Fifth Review, Pirene's Fountain, The New Verse News* ,and many others, including a poem in *The Bloomsbury Anthology of Contemporary Jewish-American Poetry*. She is editor and publisher of *Naugatuck River Review*, a journal of narrative poetry. She lives in Westfield, Massachusetts. Website: www.loridesrosiers.com
Appears in poem no.: 33

JENIL DHOLAKIA hails from the city of dreams, Mumbai, India. Writing, doodling, art, culture, lifestyle, fashion, travel are the things that interest, attract & appeal her. She loves mind-bending conversations, free association, inner monologues, films, alternative news, the internet, people, and the other side of things.
Appears in poem nos.: 131, 143

JOEL DIAS-PORTER (aka DJ Renegade) was born and raised in Pittsburgh, PA. From 1994 - 1999 he was an Individual Finalist in the National Poetry Slam, and was the 1998 and 1999 Heads Up Haiku Slam Champion. His poems have appeared in *Time Magazine, The Washington Post, Callaloo,* and *Ploughshares*; and in anthologies including: *Gathering Ground, Role Call, Def Poetry Jam, 360 Degrees of Black Poetry, Spoken Word Revolution,* and *Catch a Fire.* In 1995, He was the Furious Flower "Emerging Poet." He has performed on the *Today Show,* the films,"Slam" and "SlamNation," and on BET. A Cave Canem Fellow, his CD of jazz and poetry is *LibationSong.*
Appears in poem nos.: 30, 41, 51, 64, 67, 69, 78, 87, 93, 126

FREADA DILLON lives and writes in Micco, Florida, on the Indian River. She is a published poet and editor for several on-line and print magazines. Retired from the bustle of the work-a-day world, she is currently working on editing all the poems written from a year's worth of poem-a-day challenge. This is done between herding cats, and trying to ignore three parrots who contend with each other for demands on time and patience.
Appears in poem no.: 112

TERESA DONIGER is a DC-based licensed psychotherapist. Her clinical experience includes work with youth and adults in schools, community-based mental health agencies, as well as at psychiatric hospitals. Her approach as a therapist is eclectic and integrates key components of psychodynamic work, attachment theory, grief and loss theories, cognitive behavior therapy, and the expressive arts. She currently works within a private practice in northwest Washington, DC.
Appears in poem nos.: 135, 138, 144

TERI ELAM lives in Atlanta, Georgia. Besides the lines she has contributed to *Electronic Corpse*, she has had poems published in *The Ringing Ear: Black Poets Lean South*, *The Lion Speaks*, and *The Chemistry of Color: Poems Responding to Art*.
Appears in poem nos.: 12, 17, 23, 24, 28, 36, 41, 87, 93, 139, 144

BINA SARKAR ELLIAS is founder, editor, designer and publisher of *International Gallerie*, the award-winning global arts and ideas journal, encouraging understanding of cultural diversity. Also an art curator, poet, and fiction writer, she has received a Fellowship from the Asia Leadership Fellow Program (2007,) the Times Group Yami Women Achievers' Award (2008), and the FICCI/FLO India 2013 Award for Excellence as editor of Gallerie. She lives and works in Mumbai, India.
Appears in poem no.: 125

KWOYA FAGIN is a poet and creative writing instructor with an MFA in Creative Writing from the University of Alabama. A South Carolina native, she now lives and works in Birmingham, Alabama. She has a chapbook of poems entitled *Something of Yours* (Finishing Line Press 2010) and currently has a manuscript in progress which received support by the Rockefeller Brothers Fund. She is a graduate fellow of Cave Canem.
Appears in poem no.: 10

LATORIAL FAISON is the author of a children's book and five poetry collections, including the three-book collection, *28 Days of Poetry Celebrating Black History*. Born in rural Virginia, she was raised by grandparents and graduated University of Virginia and Virginia Tech. Her passion is promoting uplift and change through writing. Faison's work has appeared in *Southern Women's Review*, *Chickenbones*, *Kalyani*, *Poetry Quarterly*, and elsewhere. Follow her online at www.latorialfaison.com or Facebook. She currently resides in South Korea
Appears in poem nos.: 10, 126, 131, 139, 141, 144

RUPERT FIKE's collection of poems, *Lotus Buffet* (Brick Road Poetry Press) was named Finalist in the 2011 Georgia Author of the Year Awards. He has been nominated for Pushcart prizes in fiction and poetry with work appearing in *The Southern Review of Poetry*, *Rosebud*, *Natural Bridge*, *The Georgetown Review*, *A & U America's AIDS Magazine*, and others. He has a poem inscribed in a downtown Atlanta plaza, and his non-fiction, *Voices from The Farm*, is now in its second printing.
Appears in poem nos.: 3, 12, 17, 28, 44, 51, 53, 60, 63, 69, 72, 80, 87, 93, 94, 97, 105, 106, 115, 139, 144

DARNELL FINE is a multicultural thinker who facilitates education and creative writing seminars, as well as social justice workshops, around the country. In 2013, he was one of five educators across the country recognized by the Southern Poverty Law Center with the Teaching Tolerance Award for Excellence in Culturally Responsive Teaching. Currently, he resides in Brooklyn, NY, where he teaches 6th grade Humanities at a local middle school
Appears in poem nos.: 57, 60

TRACEY FOXWORTH is an author/poet, activist, and Navy veteran. While pursuing a dual degree in Criminal Justice and Journalism, she is simultaneously completing her ministerial studies. She desires nothing other than sharing her authentic self with the universe and continuing to dedicate her life to eradicate social inequalities. She splits her residence between Atlanta and the coast of South Carolina.
Appears in poem nos.: 57, 138, 139, 144

JENNIFER L. FREEMAN (Jennifer Freeman Marshall) is a native of Atlanta, Georgia. A graduate of Spelman College, Georgia State University, and Emory University, she participated in the 2005 Callaloo Creative Writing Workshop in Poetry. Citing Lucille Clifton, William Shakespeare, and Toni Morrison as inspirations, she is currently assistant professor of English and Women's Studies at Purdue University.
Appears in poem nos.: 12, 17, 33, 36, 61

HESTER L. ("LEE") FUREY has taught at the Art Institute of Atlanta for more than 15 years. Author of the chapbook, *Little Fish* (Finishing Line Press) and editor of *Dictionary of Literary Biography 345: American Radical and Reform Writers, Second Series*, Furey has published a number of poems and essays in scholarly and literary journals. A founding editor of the online journal, *eyedrum periodically*, she lives in Decatur, Georgia.
Appears in poem nos.: 12, 17, 28, 30, 32, 44, 61, 63, 67, 69, 75, 78, 80, 87

JONTERRI GADSON is author of the chapbook, *Pepper Girl* (YesYes Books, 2012). She is the recipient of scholarships/fellowships from Bread Loaf, Cave Canem, and the University of Virginia's Creative Writing MFA program. Her poetry is forthcoming or published in *Los Angeles Review, Callaloo, The Collagist, Anti-, PANK* and other journals. She currently serves as the Herbert W. Martin Post-Graduate Creative Writing Fellow at the University of Dayton in Ohio.
Appears in poem nos.: 3, 10, 19, 23, 28, 30, 36, 41, 44, 51, 57, 62, 64, 72, 75, 80, 87, 93, 97, 112, 131, 133, 141, 143

JEREMY C. GARLAND was a member of the first team to represent Baton Rouge, Louisiana, at the National Poetry Slam in 1999. He later founded and hosted an open mic called Poets Anonymous which brought touring poets from all over the country to perform feature sets in the deep south. Currently, he is a poet and writer living in Los Angeles, California, who now writes haiku and thinks about riding his bike along the beach. Visit him at www.jeremycgarland.com.
Appears in poem no.: 106

KAREN GARRABRANT is a decade-plus slam manager, poet, fanatic, host, and organizer in the Atlanta area. She partners with the nation's oldest feminist bookstore, Charis Books & More and she's been an Assistant Tournament Director, volunteer, and emcee for the Individual World Poetry Slam and the Tournament Director and competing poet in the Women of the World Poetry Slam.
Appears in poem no.: 3

JULES GIBBS lives and writes in Syracuse, NY, where the sun always shines, and everyone is kind and beautiful. She's the author of a book of poems, *Bliss Crisis*, and a chapbook, *The Bulk of the Mailable Universe*. She is currently a visiting professor of creative writing and literature at Hamilton College.
Appears in poem nos.: 1, 19, 23, 36, 53, 61, 67, 105

JON GOODE is an Emmy-nominated writer that hails from Richmond, VA, who currently resides in Atlanta, GA. He has been featured on CNN's *Black in America*, HBO's *Def Poetry*, BET's *Lyric Café* and TV One's *Verses and Flow*. His work has been showcased in radio commercials for McDonalds and print ads for Nike. His television commercial for TVLand/ Nick @ Nite earned him an Emmy nomination alongside the 2006 Promax gold award for best copyright North America. (www.jongoode.webs.com)
Appears in poem nos.: 32, 41, 53, 60, 63, 97

With a past life as a Bearded Lady performing across America, LORI GUARISCO is a dancing poet, a spoken word artist, a street performer and writer, based in Atlanta. In some of her more recent pieces, she's transformed herself into a firefighter, a superhero and a crow. She is writing her first novel, and she wants Johnny Depp to star in its film adaptation.
Appears in poem nos.: 93

MONICA A. HAND is the author of *me and Nina* (Alice James Books, 2012), shortlisted for the 2013 Hurston Wright Legacy Award. She has a MFA in Poetry and Poetry in Translation from Drew University and has attended residencies at Poets House in NYC and the Fine Arts Work Center in Provincetown, MA. A Cave Canem alumnus, she is currently, a PhD candidate in Poetry at the University of Missouri-Columbia.
Appears in poem nos.: 125, 139, 143

JERRI HARDESTY lives in the woods of Brierfield, Alabama, with husband, Kirk, also a poet. They run the nonprofit organization, NewDawnUnlimited, Inc., dedicated to poetry publishing, production, performance, promotion, preservation, and education. This includes organizing and hosting the BamaSlam Montevallo Poetry Slam as well as other poetry events around the state. Jerri has had about 300 poems published, and has won more than 600 awards and titles in both written and spoken word/performance poetry. Learn more at www.NewDawnUnlimited.com.
Appears in poem nos.: 24, 44

FRANCINE J. HARRIS' first collection, *allegiance*, reached the number one spot on the national poetry bestseller's list and was a finalist for the 2013 Kate Tufts Discovery Award and *ForeWord Review*'s Book of the Year. Her work has appeared in *Ploughshares, Rattle, Ninth Letter, Indiana Review*, and others. Originally from Detroit, she is a Cave Canem Fellow and is the Front Street Writers Writer-in-Residence in Traverse City, Michigan for the 2013/14 school year.
Appears in poem nos.: 30, 112

MISS HAZE is an Atlanta-based slam and performance poet. In 2012 she ranked in the top 10 at the Women of the World Poetry Slam and is a 4-time member of Java Monkey Slam Team. She recently ranked second in the National Poetry Slam's Head-to-Head Haiku Slam. A montage of metaphor and real life stories, her poems are intended to enlighten as well as entertain. Warning: Haze is highly addictive so proceed with caution. She is definitely worth the "trip."
Appears in poem nos.: 63, 72

M. AYODELE HEATH is author of *Otherness* (Brick Road Poetry Press) and serves as the brain of this *Electronic Corpse*. Recipient of fellowships to Caversham Centre for Artists (South Africa) and Cave Canem, he is a top individual 10-finisher at the National Poetry Slam. A graduate of the MFA in Poetry at New England College, he is a former McEver Visiting Chair in Writing at Georgia Tech. His work has appeared widely in journals and anthologies including *diode, Muzzle, Crab Orchard Review, Mississippi Review,* and India's *International Gallerie*. Virtually, he lives at www.ayospeaks.com. Physically, he lives and writes in Atlanta
Appears in poem nos.: All except 61

HARLEY HILL is a writer and poet living with her dog, Roma, by a river near Portland, Oregon.
Appears in poem nos.: 112, 115, 131, 133, 135, 144

PAIGE HOOD is an Appalachian mountain mama currently residing in Monroe, GA. She has taught high school English for 27 years. Paige dotes upon her grown children and her partner Cindy and spends much of her time feeding their several pets.
Appears in poem no.: 63

YOUNG T. HUGHLEY, JR., lives in Atlanta, Georgia. He is founder and former Chief Executive Officer of Resources for Residents and Communities of Georgia, aka Reynoldstown Revitalization Corporation (RRC). He designed a focused revitalization strategy to transform, a once disenfranchised neighborhood within the city of Atlanta into a thriving, diverse and inclusive community. Presently, he is redefining himself in terms of an encore career. To relax he enjoys writing poetry and prose as a means of creative expression.
Appears in poem no.: 78

TIFFANY G. JONES hails from Atlanta, GA, where she is one of an almost extinct population known as the "Native Atlantan." In her spare time, this amateur writer enjoys reading, acting, singing, and performing other people's poetry. In her not-so-spare time, she works for a nonprofit organization managing the financial reporting for 71 volunteer organizations. Her favorite way to relax is dancing and singing with her six year old son.
Appears in poem no.: 126

COLLIN KELLEY is an Atlanta, GA, native and author of the poetry collections *Render, After the Poison, Slow To Burn,* and *Better To Travel*. His novels include *Conquering Venus, Remain In Light* and the forthcoming *Leaving Paris*. www.collinkelley.com
Appears in poem no.: 55

JOY KMT is a prizmatic poet, artist, and space sorceress. She is a MacDowell Fellow as well as a recipient of a Heinz Endowments fellowship. Her poetry has appeared in *Check The Rhyme: An Anthology of Female Emcees and Poets, Amistad: Howard's Literary Journal, Blood Lotus, Backbone Poetry Journal, Black Girl Dangerous, The Feminist Wire,* and *Pluck! the Affrilachian Journal of Arts and Culture*. www.immaculateuniverse.com.
Appears in poem nos.: 55, 106, 133

GILLIAN LEE-FONG was born in Jamaica and is of Chinese and African heritage. She holds a BA in Creative Writing from Agnes Scott College and a M.Ed. from Columbia College. Her writing is influenced by her rich multi-cultural experience, including a career teaching English and developing educational programs for refugee and immigrant communities. Her YA novel, *Tembe*, was published in 2006. She currently lives and writes in Atlanta.
Appears in poem nos.: 12, 135

ISSA M. LEWIS' work has appeared in *Prairie Wolf Review, Looseleaf Tea, Scapegoat Review,* and *Extract(s)*. She was the winner of the 2013 Lucille Clifton Poetry Prize sponsored by Backbone Press. She makes a living by teaching composition at Davenport University and fills in the cracks with poetry. She lives and writes in Plainwell, Michigan.
Appears in poem nos.: 1, 12, 75, 97

AISHA LUMUMBA is a fiber artist residing in Atlanta, Georgia. Born in a rural suburb of Atlanta, known as McDonough, Georgia, she loves writing and quilting, which led her to write stories and books about quilting. She has more than 25 years of quilting experience, not only for practical uses, but as a form of artistic expression. Her work has been exhibited at the Birmingham Public Library and the National Black Arts Festival.
Appears in poem nos.: 17, 141, 144

KIOM MARASCHIELLO, a native of New York State, resides in Atlanta, Georgia, where she freelances in Interior Design, Fashion Consulting, and Real Estate Administration. Being a child of the 1960's "Free To Be You and Me" generation, she is both the product of and conduit to a multicultural, multi-ethnic and multi-religious family of creatives. She is the proud mother of two adult sons and new grandmother to a 4-month old granddaughter.
Appears in poem nos.: 62, 66, 72, 115

ELLYN MAYBE is a poet based in Los Angeles, California. She has performed both nationally and internationally as a solo artist and with her band at such venues as Bumbershoot, Taos Poetry Circus, South by Southwest, Lollapalooza, and the Bristol Poetry Festival. Her work has been included in many anthologies and she is the author of numerous books. She also has a critically acclaimed poetry/music album, *Rodeo for the Sheepish*. In addition to her band, her latest poetry/music project is called *Ellyn and Robbie*. ellynmaybe.com or ellynandrobbie.com
Appears in poem no.: 61

PAULA MCLAIN is author of two collections of poetry, a memoir, *Like Family*, about growing up in foster care, and a debut novel, *A Ticket to Ride*. Her second novel, *The Paris Wife*, spent a year on the *New York Times* best seller list, was named one of the best books of 2011 by *People Magazine, Chicago Tribune,* and NPR, and has been published in 35 territories internationally. Recipient of fellowships from the National Endowment for the Arts, Yaddo, and the MacDowell Colony, McLain's work has appeared in *The New York Times, Washington Post Magazine, Good Housekeeping,* and *Real Simple*. She lives with her family in Cleveland, OH.
Appears in poem no.: 19

JENN MONROE is the author of *Something More Like Love* (Finishing Line Press, 2012), executive editor of Eastern Point Press and *Extract(s): Daily Dose of Lit,* and an editor and educator for Eastern Point Lit House. Her work has been published in a number of print and online journals, and been nominated for a Pushcart Prize. She holds an MFA in Poetry from New England College and lives in New Hampshire with her husband and their young daughter
Appears in poem no.: 87

GABE MOSES is a fiction writer, poet, performer, and co-founder of the now-defunct Atlanta hip-hop collective RUUDE. He has performed everywhere from dive bars to universities to a drug rehab center, sometimes as half of the queer Jewish spoken-word duo Sexual Brisket; taught writing workshops to inner-city youth and to adults with developmental disabilities; and had his work published in numerous literary journals and anthologies. A national competitive slam poet, he was the 2013 Capturing Fire champion and is currently the Grand Slam Champion of the Art Amok Poetry Slam Team.
Appears in poem nos.: 24, 30, 44, 112, 125, 130, 135, 138, 143

LASADA LLOYD OWENS III is a monologist who resides in Columbus, GA. She serves as a missionary with her home church, Bread of Life Christian Center. Most of her monologues are original, inspired by works from Langston Hughes, Maya Angelou, family, friends, and life situations. A community supporter and advocate, she has presented monologues at various venues and television outlets throughout Columbus. She is the proud mother of three daughters and one son.
Appears in poem no.: 57, 61, 72

COLLEEN PAYTON (aka Miriam Jacobs) is a graduate of the University of Chicago and teaches college writing, literature and humanities. Her chapbook of poetry, *The Naked Prince,* was published by Fort!/Da? Books in May 2013. Jacobs/Payton writes for several publications and is the editor of *Eyedrum Periodically,* the art/literature journal of Eyedrum Art & Music Gallery, Atlanta.
Appears in poem no.: 12

AMY PENCE authored the poetry collections *Armor, Amour* (Ninebark Press, 2012) and *The Decadent Lovely* (Main Street Rag, 2010). Her hybrid work on Emily Dickinson, *[It] Incandescent,* was a finalist for Tupelo Press's Snowbound Chapbook Award and the Colorado Prize for Poetry. She's published interviews and non-fiction in *The Writer's Chronicle* and *Poets & Writers.* She lives with her husband and her daughter in Carrollton, Georgia.
Appears in poem no.: 44

CLELA REED is author of two books of poetry: *Dancing on the Rim* (Brick Road Poetry Press, 2009), *The Hero of the Revolution Serves Us Tea* (Negative Capability Press, 2014), and two chapbooks: *Bloodline* (Evening Street Press, 2009) and *Of Root and Sky* (Pudding House Publications, 2010). Her poems have appeared in *Caesura Literary Magazine, Colere Journal, Storysouth,* and elsewhere. A former English teacher and facilitator for the gifted, she recently returned from Peace Corps service in Romania where she blogged weekly about her experience. She lives and writes with her husband and a small herd of deer in her forest home near Athens, Georgia.
Appears in poem no.: 66

Robert Ricardo Reese is of mixed African-American and Korean parentage. Born in Seoul, South Korea, he grew up near the North Korean border and in all three major cities of South Korea. In 2012, he was published in *Asia Literary Review*, alongside the five-time Nobel nominee Ko Un. He currently serves as a teaching artist for San Francisco's Center for the Art of Translation.
Appears in poem no.: 19

Rick Robinson is an award winning author and political humorist.
Appears in poem no.: 57

Metta Sáma is author of *Nocturne Trio* (YesYes Books 2012) and *South of Here* (New Issues Press 2005 (published under Lydia Melvin)). Her poems, fiction, creative non-fiction, and book reviews have been published, or are forthcoming, in *Blackbird, bluestem, The Drunken Boat, Esque, hercricle, Jubilat,* and *Vinyl*, among others. Metta lives & works in Winston-Salem, North Carolina.
Appears in poem nos.: 23, 28, 30, 32, 33, 44

S. Shaw holds a BA in English with a creative writing emphasis from San Francisco State University, and a MLS from University California, Berkeley. He currently lives in Oakland, California, and works as a librarian at the San Francisco Public Library. His poems have appeared in both online and print journals such as *Missing Slate, Temenos* and *Toe Good*. He is a Cave Canem Fellow.
Appears in poem nos.: 66, 75, 80, 87, 138

April "A.P." Smith is a poet and performing artist from Atlanta, Georgia, who has been writing and speaking for over a decade. She was a member of the Art Amok Slam Team, ranked fourth out of 64 teams at the 2009 National Poetry Slam group piece finals and top 10 (out of 74 teams) at the 2010 National Poetry Slam. Smith believes "poetry is the salt in my stew; without it, life wouldn't taste right."
Appears in poem no.: 135, 141

Richard Speel has lived in Petaluma, California, since 1985. Currently 69 years old, back in the late '60s and '70s he was a founding member of a hippie commune called The Farm, located in Summertown, TN. He's always enjoyed poetry since he was a teenager and was influenced by the work of e. e. cummings. Today, he occasionally writes poems and puts them on a Facebook group he created called Today's Epiphany.

Appears in poem nos.: 51, 94, 97, 105, 106, 130

Affrilachian Poet and Cave Canem Fellow, Bianca Spriggs, is a poet and multidisciplinary artist based in Lexington, Kentucky. Recipient of a 2013 Al Smith Individual Artist Fellowship in Poetry, multiple grants from the Kentucky Foundation for Women, and a Pushcart Prize nominee, she is author of *Kaffir Lily* and *How Swallowtails Become Dragons and* Managing Editor for *pluck! The Journal of Affrilachian Art & Culture*. In partnership with the Kentucky Domestic Violence Association, she is creator of *The SwallowTale Project:creative writing for incarcerated women*. Learn more at www.biancaspriggs.com.
Appears in poem no.: 43

CHRISTINA SPRINGER is a text artist who uses poetry, dance, theatre, film and other visual expressions to perform nationally and internationally. Poems have appeared in numerous literary journals and anthologies. She has served as an Artist In Residence at the Tower Of London. As an arts organizer, she is the force behind The Svaha Paradox Salon. Springer resides in Pittsburgh where she home educates her son. www.christinaspringer.com.
Appears in poem nos.: 1, 10, 17, 23, 30, 32, 33, 36, 43, 44, 53, 55, 60, 62, 66, 72, 78, 80, 94, 105, 115, 126

MARK STATES is a spoken word artist born in Oakland, California. Long-time host of Poetry Express in Berkeley, he also was a member of the 2008 San Francisco Poetry Slam Team, and former editor of *Poetalk Magazine*. He is author of three poetry chapbooks, has appeared on radio and television, and has featured around the country. Presently, Mark lives in Charlotte, North Carolina.
Appears in poem nos.: 32, 138, 141, 143

SHARAN STRANGE is a community board member of Poetry Atlanta. She teaches at Spelman College and has also been the Bruce McEver Visiting Chair in Poetry at Georgia Tech. Her poems have appeared in numerous journals and anthologies— including *Callaloo, Agni, The American Poetry Review, Temba Tupu!, 100 Best African-American Poems,* and *The Best American Poetry*. Her poetry collection, *Ash*, was selected by Sonia Sanchez for the Barnard Women Poets Prize.
Appears in poem nos.: 10, 41, 44, 57, 78, 93, 105, 106

At the age of 48, GLORIA LAWSON SYLVESTER birthed poetry which sparked her journey in the arts. She holds a BFA in Creative Writing from Goddard College and has developed poetry workshops for public and private school students and visual art students. In 2001 she was appointed Poet Laureate of the Martin Luther King, Jr. International Chapel in Atlanta, Georgia where she currently resides.
Appears in poem nos.: 17, 36

TANAYA THOMAS is on a learning journey to pursue her interests in creative writing and circus arts. When she is not writing and dancing on stilts, she can be found exploring the arts community in her new home in Philadelphia, PA. You can find out more information at: www.about.me/tanayathomas.
Appears in poem nos.: 130, 133

JON TRIBBLE is the managing editor of *Crab Orchard Review* and series editor of the Crab Orchard Series in Poetry published by Southern Illinois University Press. His work was selected as the 2001 winner of the Campbell Corner Poetry Prize from Sarah Lawrence College, and his poems have appeared in journals and anthologies, including *Ploughshares, Poetry, Crazyhorse, Quarterly West,* and *The Jazz Poetry Anthology*. He lives in Carbondale, Illinois, and teaches at Southern Illinois University.
Appears in poem no.: 19

MARIE URSUY grew up in Freeland, Michigan, and currently resides in the heart of Indianapolis, Indiana. She received her BA degree in English from Butler University and her MFA in poetry from New England College. She has been an organizer for Robert Bly's Great Mother and New Father Conference for the past three years.
Appears in poem no.: 19

DAN VEACH is the author of *Elephant Water* and the founding editor of *Atlanta Review*. His poetry and translations have won the Willis Barnstone Translation Prize, the Independent Publisher Book Award, and the Georgia Author of the Year Award.
Appears in poem no.: 55

Kentucky Poet Laureate, FRANK X WALKER is a founder of the Affrilachian Poets and the author of six collections of poetry including, *Turn Me Loose: The Unghosting of Medgar Evers*. Voted one of the most creative professors in the south, he is the originator of the word, Affrilachia. This Lannan Poetry Fellowship Award recipient has degrees from Spalding University and University of Kentucky, were he currently serves as an Associate Professor in the English Department.
Appears in poem no.: 43

VALERIE WALLACE is a poet whose work has been published in many literary journals and anthologies. Margaret Atwood chose 10 of her poems as the winner of the 2012 Atty Award. Her work has been supported most recently by the Illinois Arts Council, Ragdale Foundation, and Midwest Writers Center. Valerie teaches workshops throughout Chicago, and is an editor with *RHINO* and the Afghan Women's Writing Project. Her chapbook *The Dictators' Guide to Good Housekeeping* is available from www.dancinggirlpress.com.
Appears in poem no.: 1

DARRIAN WESLEY is a poet and Chicago native. He has his BA degree from Bradley University. His work has been featured in *The Feminist Wire* and is forthcoming in *Word Riot*. He enjoys reading the poetry of Terrance Hayes.
Appears in poem no.: 105, 135

CANDACE G. WILEY was born in SC, graduated with her BA from Bowie State University, an HBCU in MD, her MA from Clemson University, and is finishing her MFA at the University of South Carolina. Wiley has recently finished a Fulbright Fellowship in San Basilio de Palenque, Colombia, a town founded by escaped slaves. The town has its own language and customs that trace back to the Bantu and Kikongo in West Africa. Candace is now living in Colombia and collecting narratives as the basis of a creative prose and poetry project
Appears in poem no.: 12, 32, 44, 57, 61, 64

KEITH S. WILSON is an Affrilachian Poet, Cave Canem Fellow, graduate of the Callaloo Creative Writing Workshop, and recipient of a Bread Loaf scholarship. His work has appeared, or is forth in the forthcoming, in the following journals: *American Letters & Commentary*, *32 Poems*, *Cider Press Review*, *Anti-*, *Muzzle*, *Mobius*, and *The Dead Mule School of Southern Literature*. Keith currently lives in Chicago.
Appears in poem nos.: 28, 43

L. LAMAR WILSON's *Sacrilegion* was chosen by Lee Ann Brown for the 2012 Carolina Wren Press Poetry Series and received the Independent Publishers' bronze medal in 2013. Wilson has received fellowships from Cave Canem Foundation, the Callaloo Workshops, and the Arts and Sciences Foundation at the University of North Carolina at Chapel Hill, where he is a doctoral candidate in African American and multiethnic American poetics.
Appears in poem nos.: 3, 19, 44, 53, 57, 62, 72, 78, 94, 97

ROBERT E. WOOD teaches at Georgia Tech and received a PhD at the University of Virginia. He is the author of *Some Necessary Questions of the Play, a study of Hamlet*. His poetry has appeared in *Southern Humanities Review, South Carolina Review, Quiddity, Blue Fifth Review, NDQ, Poets and Artists*, and *Prairie Schooner*. Chapbooks, *Gorizia Notebook* and *Sleight of Hand*, were published by Finishing Line Press. *The Awkward Poses of Others*, is published by WordTech.
Appears in poem nos.: 112, 130, 139

APRIL WRIGHT is a poet living in Atlanta, Georgia. She is currently working on her MFA in Creative Writing/Poetry at Queens University of Charlotte where she is an Editorial Assistant for QU Literary Journal. She has given several poetry workshops through the Atlanta Public Library and the Fulton County School System, holds several fellowships and is currently working on completing her first manuscript.
Appears in peom nos.: 106

KAREN WURL is a playwright, dramaturg, director, teacher, and semi-retired slam poet. She's spent half her life in Chicago, half her life in Atlanta, and the extra bits in Michigan, Wisconsin and Texas.
Appears in poem nos.: 9

MISSION

Thematically or by blending genres, a consistent theme has emerged. How and why do we perform ourselves on a daily basis? In any situation a person can be a: worker, color, parent, gender, artist, class, friend, educational level, lover. At all times, the layers of our identity overlap. In any human encounter, our identity intersects and/or bounces off the other people's. In any given context, whether consciously or unconsciously, everyone makes assumptions, acts on opinions or performs behavior scripted by their personal narrative.

The Svaha Paradox Salon, responds with agility to under-exposed artists whose voices are marginalized due to the way in which they are performed in the minds of the dominant culture. And together, we share the results with audiences.

Svaha Paradox Salon resumes where the Pittsburgh based organization Sun Crumbs left off in 2003. Through professional involvement In various art communities, Christina Springer seeks out artists whose exceptional work requires support from non-traditional sources. Svaha Paradox Salon provides the encouragement necessary to complete these projects.

Tax deductible contributions to Svaha Paradox Salon programming may be made through Fractured Atlas @ http://goo.gl/9l74Ec